FREUD *verbatim*

FREUD *verbatim*

Quotations and Aphorisms

=

Selected by
Hannes Etzlstorfer & Peter Nömaier

With a foreword by
Inge Scholz-Strasser

OVERLOOK DUCKWORTH
NEW YORK • LONDON

This edition first published in hardcover in the United States and the United
Kingdom in 2014 by Overlook Duckworth, Peter Mayer Publishers, Inc.
NEW YORK
141 Wooster Street
New York, NY 10012
www.overlookpress.com
For bulk and special sales please contact sales@overlookny.com,
or write us at the above address.

LONDON
30 Calvin Street
London E1 6NW
www.ducknet.co.uk
For bulk and special sales please contact sales@duckworth-publishers.co.uk,
or write us at the above address.

With the support of the Sigmund Freud Foundation

Design and typesetting: Michael Karner, www.typografie.co.at
Editing (German edition): Andreas Deppe
Translation and editing: Christopher Barber

ISBN 978-1-4683-0963-8 US
ISBN 978-0-7156-4984-8 Uk
Manufactured in the United States of America
10 9 8 7 6 5 4 3 2 1

Contents

Foreword 7
Freud Verbatim – An Introduction 12

I   The Man in Private Life 16
II   Vienna and the World 32
III   Society and Culture 44
IV   Conflict and Strife 58
V   Dream and Illusion 74
VI   Eros and Sexuality 90
VII   Science and Analysis 106
VIII   Wit and Humour 124
IX   Et Cetera 140
X   Cult and Religion 152

Appendix

Sigmund Freud – Timeline 168
Bibliography 171
List of Illustrations 173
Copyright Permissions 174
The Authors 175

"… Do not let us despise the word. After all it is a power-ful instrument; it is the means by which we convey our feel-ings to one another, our method of influencing other people. Words can do unspeakable good and cause terrible wounds. "

Sigmund Freud, *The Question of Lay Analysis*

These words from Sigmund Freud stand paradigmatically for the aim of this book, which first and foremost seeks to draw attention to the linguistic brilliance apparent everywhere in Freud's work. In presenting his fundamental theories on the human soul, Freud demonstrated an exceptional command of language and a capacity for elegant formulation that evidence his comprehensive humanist education, his passion for read-ing, and the tremendous breadth and depth of his knowledge.

Freud Verbatim is one of many fruits of the ongoing re-search and educational efforts being pursued in the rooms where Sigmund Freud lived and worked at Berggasse 19 in Vienna. The book came about through the co-operation of the Sigmund Freud Foundation, Hannes Etzlstorfer and the Brandstätter publishing house. In fulfilling its mission of fur-thering public awareness of the life and work of the founder of psychoanalysis, the Sigmund Freud Foundation presents lectures, international congresses and exhibitions at the Sigmund Freud Museum. It also operates Europe's largest psychoanalytic library, maintains a continually expanding archive of important documents in the history of psycho-analysis, and publishes scholarly works, exhibition catalogues and compilations like this one.

Every year, the Sigmund Freud Museum at Berggasse 19 in Vienna welcomes more than 70,000 people, who come from throughout the world to visit one of its most well-known addresses, where they are offered a unique opportunity to experience Freud's former medical office and residence. Here visitors can learn about the setting in which he analyzed his patients and wrote the works that would permanently transform our understanding of the human mind. The original waiting room was also the scene of the meetings of the Wednesday Psychological Society: here Freud invited a group of medical colleagues and other interested persons to discuss the burgeoning science of psychoanalysis and develop it in dialogue. Together with his family, he lived and worked for forty-seven years in these rooms, which today are open to the public as the Sigmund Freud Museum. In 1938, at the age of eighty-two, Freud was able to escape persecution at the hands of the National Socialists by fleeing to England, accompanied by his closest relatives. The last one and a half years of his life were spent in London. Shortly after the outbreak of the Second World War, on 23 September 1939, Sigmund Freud died in his house at Maresfield Gardens 20, finally succumbing to the cancer that had plagued him for many years. Today that house is the home of the Freud Museum London.

The Sigmund Freud Museum in Vienna opened its doors in 1971. From the very beginning, it was devoted to keeping alive the memory not only of Freud and his work, but also of his flight into exile – together with many other prominent intellectuals – from National Socialism. In the course of his emigration, Sigmund Freud was able to ship both his couch and his collection of antiquities to London. The couch, which during the twentieth century became the most famous symbol of psychoanalysis, is housed today in the Freud Museum London, in the house where Freud lived out his final days.

Sigmund Freud is primarily remembered as the primogenitor of current consciousness research. His work marks the beginning of modern psychiatry, and all newer forms of psychotherapy have either developed out of psychoanalysis or in critical opposition to it.

In addition to making undisputed contributions to the fields of medicine and psychiatry, Sigmund Freud, who trained as a neurologist, also has received widespread recognition for his literary talents. His work is characterized by a use of language that deviated markedly from the conventional medical style of his colleagues and went far beyond the scientific terminology of his era. His texts are rendered with a literary quality that during his lifetime earned the recognition of Nobel Prize for Literature laureates Romain Rolland and Thomas Mann. Freud himself wrote that his case histories read "like novellas," whereby this statement should certainly be seen in the context of his wry self-criticism: rarely did he express complete satisfaction with his writings. The committee of the Goethe Prize was less restrained in its enthusiasm, and took the controversial step of awarding him the Goethe Prize of the City of Frankfurt in 1930. Thus Freud stands in the company of such renowned authors as Gerhart Hauptmann, Thomas Mann, Carl Zuckmayer, Siegfried Lenz and Amos Oz. Works such as *The Interpretation of Dreams*, *Jokes and Their Relation to the Unconscious* and *Civilization and Its Discontents* demonstrate a fine sensibility for language and a timeless style that is astonishingly modern for the era. Every reader of Freud's texts is bound to encounter remarkable passages worthy of remembering and marvel at his artful use of words.

This book opens a window into Sigmund Freud's substantial and many-faceted oeuvre, and also into his private life, which is documented in numerous letters to friends and relatives. Of particular interest are his letters to his later wife Martha: Freud's complex personality is revealed from its romantic and poetic side in the rich correspondence with his fiancée, from whom he was long forced to live in separation on account of his difficult economic situation. A very different side is revealed in his letters to Wilhelm Fliess and C. G. Jung: here his humorous, cynical and vulnerable nature becomes transparent when the subject turns to his professional success, his thirst for power and his political calculation with regard to the positioning of the psychoanalytic movement.

In assembling the quotations contained in this book, the editors have not endeavoured to achieve any sort of completeness. The book was not conceived as a comprehensive overview containing excerpts from all of Freud's writings. The passages selected highlight various periods in Freud's work, and often they give insight into his own reflections on it. At the same time, the book also attempts to shed light on Freud's complex personality in the private sphere and to sketch the outlines of his ambivalent relationship to his origins, his convoluted path between atheism and Jewish identity, and his complex relationship to the city of Vienna and to the intellectual circles of Viennese society.

Ten chapters thematically group quotations culled from the written output of the scientist, cultural critic and author – and from the life of the man Sigmund Freud – who during the twentieth century revolutionized theories of the human mind and created a new method of treatment for mental suffering. *Freud Verbatim* grew out of the pleasure taken in reading Sigmund Freud, out of the confrontation with a monumental body of work, which below the surface is rife with complex and many-layered trains of thought. If the reader is stimulated to look more closely at Freud's writings and delve deeper into his world, this compendium has achieved its end.

Inge Scholz-Strasser
DIRECTOR

The biography of Sigmund Freud, perhaps more than that of any other figure in Viennese intellectual life around 1900, reveals a strikingly disparate amalgamation of traditions, mentalities, worldviews and scientific methods. Despite the intense opposition encountered by many of his ideas, the writings and statements of this first "explorer of the unconscious" exerted an irresistibly stimulating effect on contemporary thought. As the founder of psychoanalysis – and the creator of such commonly used terms as *ego*, *super-ego* and *id* – Freud has had a huge impact around the world. In Vienna, his theories soon gave rise to substantial controversy, which made his relationship to the university and the city itself increasingly difficult. The beginnings of psychoanalysis were marked not only by its competition with established psychiatry, which was based on physiological presuppositions, but also by the increasingly precarious political situation, which culminated in the collapse of the multiethnic Hapsburg Empire and in the founding of the First Austrian Republic. Virulent anti-Semitism was readily apparent in the parliament and in the political debates of everyday life. Before this background, psychoanalysis was dismissed as a Jewish science, while at the same time it was able to establish a new international forum beyond the confines of the university. Soon Freud had followers in Berlin and Zurich, and in Budapest, where the very first professorship for psychoanalysis was established, albeit only for a few weeks during the reign of the short-lived Hungarian Soviet Republic.

Freud's unbending adherence to his new conception of psychology was justified: beginning with the publication in 1900 of *The Interpretation of Dreams*, the reception of Freud's work increased in Vienna as well. It was not only within the confines of his scientific discipline that he advanced to become a much-discussed authority. Freud participated in a wide-ranging variety of discourses far beyond the hermetic world of his specialization. In positioning psychoanalysis, Freud was convinced that the science would have to pursue an interdisciplinary course, influencing and conquering other fields, but also offering its co-operation, as in the study of literature, for instance. It goes without saying that these advances were not always met with enthusiasm. Thus many of Freud's statements resonate with a defensive undertone, born out of the necessity of standing ground against subtle or overt attacks on the scientific validity of psychoanalysis.

This collection of quotes, maxims, prophecies, warnings, observations and witticisms sketches the profile of a many-faceted personality, whose interests were wide ranging. Their scope stretches from politics and polemics to religion, interpersonal relationships and humour, all of which has been distilled from Freud's numerous writings. The reader encounters a fascinating spectrum of opinions and positions, from which the contours of his personality and nature emerge. Many of his remarks reflect the issues of the times and define his standpoint before the backdrop of cultural history, but many others have lost none of their brilliant timelessness, which goes far beyond intellectual positioning. In addition to assembling passages from Freud's major works, this collection also makes use of sources that do not belong to the canon of his published writings. His letters, in particular, are a rich font of personal information and amusing quips. Published correspondences edited by Jeffrey Moussaieff Mason, Ernst and Lucie Freud, William McGuire, Walter Boehlich, Eva Brabant, Albrecht Hirschmüller and Michael Schröter have provided much material. This volume owes many of its most memorable passages to the fruits of their labour.

Organized into ten thematic chapters, this compilation of aphorisms and quotations provides a representative look into Freud's work, which any reader can quickly begin to explore. Thus the quote, by its nature only a part, nonetheless speaks for the whole.

Why do we so often turn to the quote? Often we find the complex world of thought behind scientific or artistic statements reduced therein to a spark of insight, which illuminates its surroundings, making them more understandable. Particularly in the more recent past, which is so rich in biographical documentation, the cogent statements of key figures represent a valuable source of information for those seriously interested in exploring an epoch and its *Zeitgeist*. Such penetrating comments – which often reveal more about the peculiarities of an era or the facets of a personality than minutely detailed analyses – have long provided an indispensable treasure trove of quotes from which speeches, texts and exhibitions derive their most pointed messages. Since the flourishing of Hellenic and Roman culture, in which Freud saw many of his theories prefigured, aphorisms have served as a vehicle for the concise formulation of a thought, judgement or piece of wisdom. Freud himself delivers perhaps the most convincing legitimization of our endeavour: "That which is true is fully deserving of being shared."

Our idea of creating a Freud florilegium would have had little chance of reaching the press without the assistance of influential supporters. Inge Scholz-Strasser, Chairwoman of the Sigmund Freud Foundation, soon recognized the need for such a publication and made essential contributions to the project's success. Christian Brandstätter took up the idea with great verve and found a place for it in the bountiful agenda of his publishing house, and we would like to express our sincere thanks to him and his team. We would also like to thank Christopher Barber for translating and editing, and for his insightful comments. Lastly, our thanks go to the following people and organizations for facilitating the use of copyrighted material: Karen Pelaez at Harvard University Press, Rachel Atkinson at Penguin Books, Catherine Trippett at Random House, Stephanie Ebdon and Tom Roberts at Sigmund Freud Copyrights.

Hannes Etzlstorfer & Peter Nömaier

I

THE MAN
IN PRIVATE LIFE

"Friends are after all
the most precious acquisitions ..."

A neatly trimmed beard, well dressed, upright posture. His glowering eyes analytically focused on the beholder, the ever-present cigar in hand. Sigmund Freud is known throughout the world in countless reproductions of such images. The most famous of these photos was shot by his son-in-law Max Halberstadt, which gives rise to an interesting subtext: the person so pierced by Freud's scrutinizing gaze is the husband of his beloved daughter Sophie.

Freud's relationship to Halberstadt was better than the photograph would lead one to expect, as is demonstrated by a touching letter written on the occasion of the couple's engagement. In the letter, Freud ceremoniously puts Sophie in Halberstadt's hands, expressing his affection for his daughter and his trust in his newly won son-in-law. The marriage began well in 1913, but it was abruptly ended by Sophie's tragic death seven years later at the age of twenty-seven. Freud, who had been hit hard by his father's death in 1896, had great difficulty in overcoming this loss. In the letters surrounding these tragic blows of fate, an emotional side of Freud's personality emerges that to this day has remained little known. According to his biographers, Freud was distanced in his personal relationships. In his letters, however, he could be loving, confiding and supportive, and some written in his younger years even reveal impassioned outbreaks of feeling. The letters to his fiancée Martha Bernays, written during their engagement when she was living in Hamburg, are replete with passages poetically expressing his love and yearning. An intensive correspondence evolved with Martha over the years, and with her sister Minna Bernays as well, who after the death of her fiancé moved into the family apartment at Berggasse 19, living there until the end of her life as the unwed "Aunt Minna".

Alongside his intensive work life, which was characterized by a daily schedule filled with analysis sessions followed by work at his desk until late into the night, Freud found little time for other pursuits. Nonetheless, his enthusiasm for travelling is well documented, and weekly meetings to play tarok (a card game) as well as occasional cafe visits were his most frequent recreation. His brother Alexander Freud was an important partner in these leisure activities. Ten years younger than Sigmund and also academically distinguished – as a professor at the forerunner of the Vienna Economic University – he was a confidant, travel companion and tarok partner. According to the biographical literature, life alongside young Sigmund was often difficult for the Freud siblings: precocious and intellectually gifted, he soon developed the ambition that remained characteristic throughout his life. Many of his letters to Martha and to the friend of his youth Eduard Silberstein provide insight into his education. Called "Golden Sigi" by his mother, Freud was at the head of his class for many years, and he made no secret of his feelings of superiority.

Freud's development from a young physician into a recognized theoretician is well documented in his correspondence with Wilhelm Fliess. Beginning in 1887, Freud exchanged opinions on theoretical, medical and private issues with the Berlin doctor, and a close friendship soon developed between them. In these letters Freud is astonishingly candid and approachable, often showing a great sense of humour. Freud openly wrote of his cocaine consumption, as he did in his letters to Martha – at the time no laws prohibited the narcotic, and thus he saw no reason to keep his use of it a secret. The friendship between the two doctors was primarily based in the lack of recognition their revolutionary theories received in the world of established medicine. Born in 1858, Fliess was an ear, nose and throat specialist in Berlin, where he also engaged in studies of cyclical processes of illness and health. Although he served as president of the German Academy of Sciences, he was never able to achieve any significant scientific success. Freud not only entrusted Fliess with reading his manuscripts: he also shared intimate aspects of his life and emotions with him. Thus his letters relate his sorrow at the death of his father and his joy at the birth of his children. With time Freud and Fliess came into conflict over scientific issues, which strained their friendship and eventually led them to break off contact. In 1904, after years without any exchange of letters, Fliess accused Freud of having communicated his theories to the controversial young Austrian philosopher Otto Weininger, who attracted great attention in presenting them as his own. The former friends' alienation became a spiteful break.

From 1923 onward, Freud's life was overshadowed by his affliction with cancer. Left for weeks in a state of uncertainty by his doctors, Freud himself knew quite well what the tumour on his jaw would mean. Having until then paid little heed to his health, he was forced to adhere to a strict regimen, whereby quitting smoking (up to twenty cigars per day) became a drawn-out struggle. Freud underwent a total of thirty-three operations on his jaw and palate. Undaunted, he continued work on his writings, although in public his daughter Anna increasingly became his mouthpiece: the operations and the oral prosthesis he was forced to wear made it difficult for him to speak, and thus she read his papers at international conferences, becoming what he would later refer to as his "Antigone". It was also her arrest by the Gestapo following the National Socialist take-over in 1938 that finally convinced Freud to leave Vienna, at the age of eighty-two, and face the ordeal of fleeing to England. Marie Bonaparte, Princess of Denmark and Greece, played a key role in facilitating the move. Passages from Freud's correspondence with her bear witness to the close relationship that she had developed with the family over the years. On 23 September 1939, marked by age and his struggle with cancer, Freud voluntarily ended his life with the aid of his trusted physician Max Schur.

=

1   "Friends are after all the most precious acquisitions ..."

2   " I don't deny that I like to be right."

3   "Anyone who writes a biography is committed to lies, concealments, hypocrisy, flattery and even to hide his own lack of understanding, for biographical truth does not exist, and if it did we could not use it."

4   "... Not all men are worthy of love."

5   "It is impossible to escape the impression that people commonly use false standards of measurement — that they seek power, success and wealth for themselves and admire them in others, and that they underestimate what is of true value in life."

6   "With the help of the necessary boldness and lack of conscience, it is not difficult to amass a large fortune, and for such services a title will of course be a suitable reward."

7   "I cannot imagine who invented the tale about women's dresses being so expensive that a man simply dare not marry!"

8   "If it had been a son, I would have sent you the news by telegram, because he would have carried your name. Since it turned out to be a little daughter by the name of Anna, she is being introduced to you belatedly."

"Annerl *(Anna Freud)* is dully voracious and has six unob- 9
served teeth, thanks to her unscientific mother."

"It cannot have remained concealed from you that fate has 10
granted me as compensation for much that has been denied
me the possession of a daughter *(Anna Freud)* who, in tragic circumstances, would not have fallen short of Antigone."

"How beautifully Nature has arranged it that as soon as a 11
child comes into the world it finds a mother ready to take
care of it!"

"The necessities of life and the 'the unvaried, still returning 12
hour of duty' – they are a source of comfort in this time of
sadness."

"We are threatened with suffering from three directions: 13
from our own body, which is doomed to decay and dissolu-
tion and which cannot even do without pain and anxiety as
warning signals; from the external world, which may rage
against us with overwhelming and merciless forces of destruction; and finally from our relations to other men. The
suffering which comes from this last source is perhaps more
painful to us than any other."

"Happiness, however, is something essentially subjective." 14

15 "We are so made that we can derive intense enjoyment only from a contrast and very little from a state of things. Thus our possibilities of happiness are already restricted by our constitution."

16 "In the last fifteen years I have never willingly sat for a photographer, because I am too vain to countenance my physical deterioration."

17 "Two cigars a day – thereby one recognizes the nonsmoker!"

18 "I need a lot of cocaine. Also, I have started smoking again, moderately, in the last two to three weeks, since the nasal conviction has become evident to me. I have not observed any ensuing disadvantage."

19 "White tie and white gloves, even a fresh shirt, a careful brushing of my last remaining hair, and so on. A little cocaine, to untie my tongue."

20 "My father seems to be on his deathbed; he is at times confused and is steadily shrivelling up, moving towards pneumonia and a fateful date."

21 "I myself still have a mother, and she bars my way to the longed-for rest, to eternal nothingness; I somehow could not forgive myself if I were to die before her."

"It is hard, after all, to succeed in satisfying each other completely; one misses, and is critical of, something in everyone." 22

"In my life, as you know, woman has never replaced the comrade, the friend." 23

"I am gradually becoming accustomed to the wine; it seems like an old friend." 24

"On Saturday evenings I look forward to an orgy of tarok, and every second Tuesday I spend among my Jewish brethren, to whom I recently gave another lecture." 25

"I know I am someone, without needing continual recognition." 26

"I can scarcely detail for you all the things that resolve themselves into excrement for me (a new Midas!). It fits in completely with the theory of internal stinking. Above all, money itself." 27

"To be healthy is wonderful if one isn't condemned to be alone." 28

"I consider it a great misfortune that nature has not granted me that indefinite something which attracts people." 29

30 "I believe people see something alien in me, and the real reason for this is that in my youth I was never young, and now that I am entering the age of maturity, I cannot mature properly."

31 "I am not even very gifted; my whole capacity for work probably springs from my character and from the absence of outstanding intellectual weaknesses."

32 "I have examined myself thoroughly and come to the conclusion that I don't need to change much."

33 "Not long ago I saw Schnitzler's *Paracelsus;* I was amazed at how much a poet knows."

34 "Now you too have reached your sixtieth birthday, while I, six years older, am approaching the limit of life and may soon expect to see the end of the fifth act of this rather incomprehensible and not always amusing comedy."

35 "I think I have avoided you from a kind of reluctance to meet my double."

36 "Indeed, I believe that fundamentally your nature is that of an explorer of psychological depths, as honestly impartial and undaunted as anyone has ever been, and that if you had not been so constituted, your artistic abilities, your gift for language and your creative power would have had free rein and made you into a writer of greater appeal to the taste of the masses."

"In my old age I seem to be developing a lot of talent for the enjoyment of life." 37

"Four weeks ago I had one of my normal operations, followed by unusually violent pain, so that I had to cancel my work for twelve days, and I lay with pain and hot-water bottles on the couch which is meant for others." 38

"A human being is so miserable when all he wants is to stay alive." 39

"After all, one does not want to die immediately or completely." 40

"How often do I not envy Einstein the youth and energy which enable him to support so many causes with such vigour. I am not only old, feeble and tired, but I am also burdened with heavy financial obligations." 41

"Of course I am still not very enthusiastic about celebrations, especially when they are there to remind one how old one has become." 42

"The idea of peaceful old age seems as much of a legend as that of happy youth." 43

"A crust of indifference is slowly creeping up around me; a fact I state without complaining. It is a natural development, a way of beginning to be inorganic. The 'detachment of old age', I think it is called." 44

45 "Does it make any sense for a man of my age to try and fill his library? At best in the interest of his heirs."

46 "I am relieved of material worries, surrounded by popularity which is distasteful to me, and involved in enterprises which rob me of the time and leisure for calm scientific work."

47 "I do not want to be eighty-nine years old. That is cruel."

48 "The times are gloomy; fortunately it is not my job to brighten them."

49 "I am not even allowed to climb a few stairs; in other words, I'm not up to the strains of an extended journey. Furthermore, I am tied down to my surgeon, who has been keeping me alive for the last fourteen years. Thus I will have to hold out here, even if the clouds on the horizon continue to darken. In the rather unlikely worst case that life and liberty become threatened, a short car ride via Pressburg *(now Bratislava, just over the Slovakian border)* will have carry me to safety."

50 "All of our things have arrived undamaged. The objects of my collection have much more space, and they make more of an impression than they did in Vienna. Of course the collection is dead now – nothing more will be added to it – and its owner is more or less just as dead."

51 " The rest – you will know what I mean – is silence."

"The costs of my funeral should be kept *as low as possible*:   52
simplest category, *no* eulogies, announcement *ex post facto*. I
promise not to be hurt at the absence of any and every 'piety'.
If it is convenient and cheap: cremation. Should I be famous
at the time of my death – one never knows – that should not
make any difference."

"I see a cloud of disaster passing over the world, even over   53
my own little world."

—

SOURCES

1 *Freud/Jung*, 1991, p. 194, 19 June 1910
2 *Freud/Jung*, 1991, p. 252, 31 Dec. 1911
3 *Freud/Zweig*, 1970, p. 127, 31 May 1936
4 *Civilization*, 1961, p. 102
5 *Civilization*, 1961, p. 64
6 *Jokes*, 1961, p. 43
7 *Letters*, 1961, p. 149, 6 June 1885, to Martha Bernays
8 *Freud/Fliess*, 1985, p. 153, 3 Dec. 1895
9 *Freud/Fliess*, 1985, p. 196, 12 Aug. 1896
10 *Freud/Zweig*, 1970, p. 66, 25 Feb. 1934
11 *Jokes*, 1961, p. 60
12 *Briefe an die Kinder*, 2010, p. 555, 26 Jan. 1920, to Max Halberstadt
13 *Civilization*, 1961, p. 77
14 *Civilization*, 1961, p. 89
15 *Civilization*, 1961, p. 76f
16 *Freud/Jung*, 1991, p. 81, 19 Sept. 1907
17 *Freud/Fliess*, 1985, p. 63, 11 Dec. 1893
18 *Freud/Fliess*, 1985, p. 132, 12 June 1895

19   *Letters,* 1961, p. 193, 18 Jan. 1886, to Martha Bernays

20   *Freud/Fliess,* 1985, p. 199, 29 Sept. 1896

21   *Letters,* 1961, p. 392, 1 Dec. 1929, to Max Eitingon

22   *Letters,* 1961, p. 372, 20 Nov. 1926, to Ernest Jones

23   *Freud/Fliess,* 1985, p. 447, 7 Aug. 1901

24   *Freud/Fliess,* 1985, p. 357, 27 June 1899

25   *Freud/Fliess,* 1985, p. 404, 23 March 1900

26   *Letters,* 1961, p. 105, 19 April 1884, to Martha Bernays

27   *Freud/Fliess,* 1985, p. 288, 22 Dec. 1897

28   *Letters,* 1961, p. 142, 29 April 1885, to Martha Bernays

29   *Letters,* 1961, p. 199, 27 Jan. 1886, to Martha Bernays

30   *Letters,* 1961, p. 202, 2 Feb. 1886, to Martha Bernays

31   *Letters,* 1961, p. 202, 2 Feb. 1886, to Martha Bernays

32   *Letters,* 1961, p. 226, 3 May 1889, to Josef Breuer

33   *Freud/Fliess,* 1985, p. 348, 19 March 1899

34   *Letters,* 1961, p. 339, 14 May 1922, to Arthur Schnitzler

35   *Letters,* 1961, p. 339, 14 May 1922, to Arthur Schnitzler

36   *Letters,* 1961, p. 340, 14 May 1922, to Arthur Schnitzler

37   *Letters,* 1961, p. 276, 25 Sept. 1908, to the family

38   *Freud/Zweig,* 1970, p. 158, 21 March 1938

39   *Letters,* 1961, p. 171, 14 Aug. 1885, to Martha Bernays

40   *Freud/Fliess,* 1985, p. 74, 21 May 1894

41   *Freud/Zweig,* 1970, p. 6, 20 Feb. 1929

42   *Briefe an die Kinder,* 2010, p. 322, 8 May 1921, to Ernst Freud

43   *Letters,* 1961, p. 336, 20 Dec. 1921, to Ernst and Lucie Freud

44   *Letters,* 1961, p. 360, 10 May 1925, to Lou Andreas-Salomé

45   *Letters,* 1961, p. 380, 12 May 1928, to Havelock Ellis

46   *Letters,* 1961, p. 338, 24 Jan. 1922, to Max Eitingon

47   *Briefe,* 1968, p. 219, 8 March 1886, to Rosa Freud

48   *Letters,* 1961, p. 425, 2 May 1935, to Arnold Zweig

49   *Briefe an die Kinder,* 2010, p. 440, 22 Feb. 1938, to Ernst Freud

50   Letter to Margaret Stonborough-Wittgenstein, Sigmund Freud
     Archive, Vienna

51   *Letters,* 1961, p. 442, 19 April 1938, to Alexander Freud

52   *Briefe an die Kinder,* 2010, p. 214, 31 Jan. 1919

53   *Freud/Zweig,* 1970, p. 101, 13 Feb. 1935

II

VIENNA AND THE WORLD

"Vienna weighs upon me and perhaps
more than is right."

S igmund Freud was born in 1856 in the Moravian town of Freiberg (Czech: Příbor), which at the time was part of the Hapsburg Empire. In 1859 his father decided to move, and after a short stay in Leipzig the family settled in Vienna, where Sigmund attended the *Gymnasium*. Freud characterized his childhood in Freiberg as a happy one, but his relationship to Vienna was ambivalent from early on.

At the latest during Freud's student years, his wonder at the beauty of Vienna's landscape and its buildings was offset by his aversion toward its society, a sentiment typical of many of the Viennese. Most of all, his attitude was a product of the anti-Semitism he had confronted since his youth. For Freud, Austrian politics was a source of continual indignation; it provided the inspiration for numerous quips, directed at both the overtly anti-Semitic Mayor Karl Lueger and the Hapsburgs. From his standpoint, the monarchy's court ceremonial and opulently staged public events were ridiculous and anachronistic. Even in his sleep he could not avoid the omnipresent aristocracy – as can be read in *The Interpretation of Dreams* in his dream of Count Thun.

He considered the sexual morality in Vienna freer than in many other cities, which led him to reject the thought expressed by many contemporaries that psychoanalysis could only have developed in Vienna. Actually, he often stressed that Vienna had done nothing to promote the growth of psychoanalysis, chafing at the lack of support it received from the university and the medical world.

Hence, from the very beginning, Freud was internationally oriented in the development of psychoanalysis. This corresponded with his personal predisposition: his life was characterized by several protracted stays abroad and by frequent travelling. In his younger years, it was an amorous interest that often occasioned his travels: Martha Bernays, later Martha Freud, lived in the North German town of Wandsbek, now part of Hamburg, and Freud visited her as often as he could. As a student he was often forced to borrow money for the trip, particularly from his mentor Josef Breuer. Two research grants enabled the young doctor to leave Vienna for longer periods of time: in Trieste he studied the sexual organs of eels, and in Paris he spent a semester at the Salpêtrière under the famed neurologist Jean-Martin Charcot. Although his admiration for Charcot was immense, the French in general made a rather poor impression. Nonetheless, he would visit the country on numerous occasions.

Freud liked to spend his summers vacationing in the mountains: hiking and mushroom gathering in the Alpine region surrounding Reichenau, a small town two hours' train ride from Vienna, provided the ideal recreation from his work. The family holidays there – or on occasion in the mountains of Austria's Salzkammergut or Bavaria's Berchtesgaden – usually lasted for several weeks, during which Freud worked diligently on his writings in the evenings. Substantial sections of numerous key texts were first set to paper in his Alpine summer residences.

The Mediterranean world also exerted a strong attraction on Freud, particularly on account of his keen interest in antiquity. Italy was his destination of preference, as is evidenced by his several stays in Rome and trips to Sicily and the Italian Alps. On his travels he was generally accompanied by his wife Martha, his sister-in-law Minna or his brother Alexander.

Congresses and lecture tours kept Freud travelling throughout Europe until an advanced age. To stress the movement's internationality, psychoanalytic congresses were strategically spread around the continent. In 1909 Freud was accompanied by C. G. Jung and other psychoanalysts on a trip to the USA for a series of lectures. The journey was motivated both by economic ends and by the desire to increase awareness of his work in America. Freud's visit was treated as a very important occasion in the United States, and he was of the opinion that the American scientists were paying him the respect that he had unjustly been denied in Europe – particularly in Vienna. His feelings about the country itself were less enthusiastic, and he decided, despite numerous offers, never to undertake another trip to the USA. In his later years, Freud's illness forced him to curtail his travelling, although it also caused him to visit Berlin for treatment on a number of occasions.

In 1938 Adolf Hitler announced the annexation of Austria by Nazi Germany. Freud had to flee into exile and departed on his last major trip, boarding the Orient Express and leaving Vienna permanently to die in freedom. Upon arriving in London on 6 June, after a short stay in Paris, he admitted that he felt a certain wistfulness for Vienna, the "prison ... I still loved greatly."

=

"Vienna weighs upon me and perhaps more than is right."   1

"Otherwise Vienna is Vienna, that is, extremely disgusting."   2

"I dread Vienna, and I would dread it three times over, re-   3
turning from Berlin."

"The feeling of triumph on being liberated is too strongly   4
mixed with sorrow, for in spite of everything I still greatly
loved the prison from which I have been released. The en-
chantment of the new surroundings (which make one shout
'Heil Hitler'!) is blended with discontent caused by little peculiarities of the strange environment. The happy anticipa-
tions of a new life are dampened by the question: How long
will a fatigued heart be able to accomplish any work? Under
the impact of the illness on the floor above me – I haven't
been allowed to see her *(Minna)* yet – the pain in the heart
turns into an unmistakable depression."

"I expect you know that the English, after having created the   5
notion of comfort, refused to have anything more to do with
it."

"May God rain down upon France a few healthy doses of   6
hellfire!"

"The number of things one has to renounce! And instead one   7
is overwhelmed with honours (such as the Freedom of the
City of Vienna), for which one would never have lifted a
finger."

8   "The suggestion is that psycho-analysis, and in particular its assertion that the neuroses are traceable to disturbances in sexual life, could only have originated in a town like Vienna – in an atmosphere of sensuality and immorality foreign to other cities – and that it is simply a reflection, a projection into theory, as it were, of these peculiar Viennese conditions. Now I am certainly no local patriot; but this theory about psycho-analysis always seems to me quite exceptionally senseless – so senseless, in fact, that I have sometimes been inclined to suppose that the reproach of being a citizen of Vienna is only a euphemistic substitute for another reproach which no one would care to put forward openly."

9   "The Viennese are no more abstinent and no more neurotic than the inhabitants of any other capital city. There is rather less embarrassment – less prudery – in regard to sexual relationships than in the cities of the West and North which are so proud of their chastity."

10   "As if the most useless things in the world were not arranged in the following order: shirt collars, philosophers, and monarchs."

11   "I thought of the phrase about the great gentlemen who had taken the trouble to be born, and of the *droit du Seigneur* which Count Almaviva tried to exercise over Susanna. I thought, too, of how our malicious opposition journalists made jokes over Count Thun's name, calling him instead 'Count Nichtsthun' *(Count Do-nothing)*. Not that I envied him. He was on the way to a difficult audience with the Em-

peror, while I was the real Count Do-nothing – just off on my holidays."

"Recently in a daytime fantasy (of which I am by no means 12 free as yet) I hurled these words at His Excellency, the Minister of Education: 'You cannot frighten me. I know that I shall still be a university lecturer when you have long ceased to be called minister.'"

"In short, one manages; and life is generally known to be very 13 difficult and very complicated and, as we say in Vienna, there are many roads to the Central Cemetery."

"Billroth's *(a renowned Viennese surgeon)* death is the event 14 of the day around here. How enviable not to have outlived oneself."

"Hungary, so near geographically to Austria, and so far from 15 it scientifically, has produced only one collaborator, S. Ferenczi, but one that indeed outweighs a whole society."

"Most of my followers and co-workers at the present time 16 came to me by way of Zurich, even those who were geographically much nearer to Vienna than to Switzerland."

"Among European countries, France has hitherto shown it- 17 self the least disposed to welcome psycho-analysis, although useful work in French by A. Maeder of Zurich has provided easy access to its theories."

18   "When you go into a shop here, everything dwelling there cries out with one voice, *'Monsieur!'*, only to then deceive you with a cold and impertinent smile."

19   "They are people given to psychical epidemics, historical mass-convulsions, and they haven't changed since Victor Hugo wrote *Notre Dame*."

20   "The *grande nation* cannot face the idea that it could be defeated in war. Ergo it was not defeated; the victory does not count. It provides an example of mass paranoia and invents the delusion of a betrayal. The alcoholic will never admit to himself that he has become impotent through drink. However much alcohol he can tolerate, he cannot tolerate this insight. So his wife is to blame – delusions of jealousy and so on."

21   "Sicily is the most beautiful part of Italy and has preserved unique fragments of ancient Greece, infantile reminiscences that make it possible to infer the nuclear complex."

22   "The most difficult thing in Rome, where nothing is easy, is shopping."

23   "Palermo was an incredible feast, something in which one really shouldn't indulge alone."

24   "Breslau also plays a role in my childhood memories. At the age of three years I passed through the station when we moved from Freiberg to Leipzig, and the gas flames which

I saw for the first time there reminded me of spirits burn-
ing in hell."

"I am sitting here in the Tatra, shivering. If there is anything   25
like a cold paradise, this is it, but in paradise it must be warm,
even rather hot, and the wind must blow warm, not like this
cold storm which tries to carry off one's notepaper while one
writes."

"Deep within me, although overlaid, there continues to live   26
the happy child from Freiberg, the first-born son of a youth-
ful mother, the boy who received from this air, from this soil,
the first indelible impressions."

"In the restaurant 'Stadt Freiberg' I sat among the Leipzig   27
Philistines, listening to their talk and watching their faces.
They talk just as much rot as the people at home, but they
look more human; I don't see so many grotesque and an-
imal-like faces, so many deformed skulls and potato noses
here."

"I don't believe that Germany will show any sympathy for   28
our work until some bigwig has solemnly given his stamp of
approval. The simplest way might be to arouse the interest
of Kaiser Wilhelm – who of course understands everything."

"Our reception in London was a very cordial one. The more   29
serious papers have been printing brief and friendly lines of
welcome. All kinds of fuss is bound to be in store for us."

30 "Everything here is rather strange, difficult, and often bewildering, but all the same it is the only country we can live in, France being impossible on account of the language."

31 "I have already declined two invitations to travel to America for lectures and to treat patients. It would surely be a grinding ordeal with little chance of profit."

32 "Quite against my will I must live like an American: no time for the libido."

33 "You know, when one is travelling to America the journey as far as Stockerau *(an hour's train ride from Vienna)* passes very quickly, but from there time begins to drag. And the return journey is the same, the last bit from Stockerau seems so slow."

34 "It is impossible to talk of the land unless one is a poet or quotes others."

=

SOURCES

1 *Letters*, 1961, p. 212, 10 March 1886, to Martha Bernays
2 *Freud/Fliess*, 1985, p. 409, 16 April 1900
3 *Freud/Fliess*, 1985, p. 371, 11 Sept. 1899
4 *Letters*, 1961, p. 446, 6 June 1938, to Max Eitingon
5 *Letters*, 1961, p. 390, 28 July 1929, to Lou Andreas-Salomé
6 *Freud/Minna Bernays*, 2005, p. 210, 28 July 1889
7 *Letters*, 1961, p. 350, 13 May 1924, to Lou Andreas-Salomé

8   *History of the Movement,* 1961, p. 39 f.

9   *History of the Movement,* 1961, p. 40

10   *Freud/Silberstein,* p. 52, 22 Aug. 1874

11   *Dreams,* 1961, p. 209

12   *Freud/Fliess,* 1985, p. 293, 4 Jan. 1898

13   *Freud/Fliess,* 1985, p. 22, 28 May 1888

14   *Freud/Fliess,* 1985, p. 66, 7 Feb. 1894

15   *History of the Movement,* 1961, p. 33

16   *History of the Movement,* 1961, p. 27

17   *History of the Movement,* 1961, p. 32

18   *Freud/Minna Bernays,* 2005, p. 118, 18 Oct. 1885

19   *Letters,* 1961, p. 188, 3 Dec. 1885, to Minna Bernays

20   *Freud/Fliess,* 1985, p. 110, 24 Jan. 1895

21   *Letters,* 1961, p. 198, 24 Sept. 1910, to C. G. Jung

22   *Letters,* 1961, p. 260, 21 Sept. 1907, to the family

23   *Letters,* 1961, p. 280, 15 Sept. 1910, to Martha Freud

24   *Freud/Fliess,* 1985, p. 285, 3 Dec. 1897

25   *Letters,* 1961, p. 319, 13 July 1917, to Lou Andreas-Salomé

26   *Letters,* 1961, p. 408, 25 Oct. 1931, to the mayor of Příbor

27   *Letters,* 1961, p. 79, 12 Dec. 1883, to Martha Bernays

28   *Freud/Jung,* p. 70, 18 Aug. 1907

29   *Letters,* 1961, p. 445, 6 June 1939, to Max Eitingon

30   *Letters,* 1961, p. 453, 4 Oct. 1938, to Marie Bonaparte

31   *Briefe an die Kinder,* 2010, p. 319, 16 Jan. 1921, to Ernst Freud

32   *Freud/Jung,* p. 162, 17 Oct. 1909

33   *Letters,* 1961, p. 157 f., 6 June 1885, to Martha Bernays

34   *Letters,* 1961, p. 249, 17 Sept. 1905, to Alexander Freud

III

SOCIETY
AND CULTURE

"Generally speaking, our civilization
is built up on the suppression
of instincts."

What holds our society together? Which principles govern human coexistence and which factors promote the development of civilizations? When Freud sets out to answer such questions, he generally takes a very expansive and speculative approach, as he does in the essay *Civilization and Its Discontents*, which was published in 1930. In this work, Freud was returning – via a lifelong path of intellectual development traversing the natural sciences, medicine and psychotherapy – to the quandary of human civilization's origins, which had already preoccupied him in his youth.

It was not, however, only in youth and in old age that Freud addressed issues of society and culture: they permeate all of his scientific work. In *Civilization and Its Discontents*, Freud distilled many of these thoughts in his analysis of the antagonism between civilization and the life of instinct. The human being, as a "tireless pleasure-seeker", is in his actions guided by two fundamental principles: avoiding pain and "unpleasure", and seeking the fulfilment of drives so as to achieve pleasure. Generally the first principle – the avoidance of pain – remains dominant, although every human being very soon learns through experience that the realities of life severely limit the fulfilment of both of these primal aims. Pain and suffering are inescapable, while happiness can only be achieved temporarily: pleasure soon fades when the stimulus from which it derives is no longer new. To achieve happiness, however, the civilized human being is even ready to sacrifice security.

Civilization also involves power: the balance between the demands of the individual and of the society depends on the latter's cultural makeup. In his theory of society, Freud addresses the question of the monopoly of power, contrasting the power of the individual, which often enough is defamed as "brute force", with the power of the group, which appears as "right". For Freud, the decisive civilizational step is taken when a society succeeds in supplanting the power of the individual with the power of the group. Before this background, Freud develops his analysis of society and culture, which is marked by concepts such as repression, sublimation and the "cultural super-ego". The tenor of Freud's thinking is revealed in his supposition that every form of civilization must force the individual to suppress certain drives harmful to the coexistence of the group.

Here Freud makes the observation that in the family it was the man who could live out the continual urges of his sex drive, while the woman's most pressing responsibility became the protection of the child as part of herself. Need and the obligations of productive work made it necessary to organize into groups to improve the toils of life. This process made evident the contradiction between the woman's interests and the duties of civilization: according to Freud, it was the men who acted to meet the growing duties of the civilized group and were forced to divert their instinctual energy to the corresponding objectives. The transformation occurred at the expense of the woman, who not only felt disadvantaged but also began to assume an increasingly hostile stance toward civilization. Thus Freud brings to light the apparent contradiction between nature and culture. While he initially associated the tension between the desire for pleasure and the sublimation of drives (i.e. moral prohibitions) with the sex drive, his later work shifted the connection toward aggressive and self-destructive drives.

Freud also addressed the demands of civilization and the question of the utility of culture. In doing so, he noted the special position of beauty, cleanliness and order among the demands of civilization. Freud saw beauty – which he classified as unnecessary – as a confirmation that one should not evaluate civilization solely from the perspective of utility: among civilizational interests beauty occupies a key position. Freud hurried to emphasize that uncleanness of every sort must appear irreconcilable with civilization. The benefit of order, he maintained, is that it ensures the human being the best exploitation of space and time while simultaneously conserving psychical energies.

=

"Generally speaking, our civilization is built up on the suppression of instincts." 1

"We soon realize that what we know to be useless, but expect civilization to value, is beauty." 2

"Civilized man has traded in a portion of his chances of happiness for a certain measure of security." 3

"Squalor of any kind seems to us incompatible with civilization." 4

"Writing is in origin the language of the absent, the house a substitute for the womb – one's first dwelling place, probably still longed for, where one was safe and felt so comfortable." 5

"The fact that civilization is not concerned solely with utility is demonstrated by the example of beauty, which we insist on including among the interests of civilization." 6

"Beauty, cleanliness and order plainly have a special place among the requirements of civilization." 7

"We grant that higher culture and education have a great influence on the development of repression ..." 8

"When primitive man had discovered that he had it in his own hands – quite literally – to improve his earthly lot by working, it could no longer be a matter of indifference to him whether 9 someone else was working with him or against him. This person now acquired for him the value of a fellow-worker, and it was useful to him if they both lived together."

10   "Human beings are simply 'tireless pleasure-seekers'."

11   "The benefits of order are undeniable; it enables people to make the best use of space and time, while sparing their mental forces."

12   "Communal life becomes possible only when a majority comes together that is stronger than any individual and presents a united front against every individual. The power of the community then pits itself, in the name of 'right', against the power of the individual, which is condemned as 'brute force'. The replacement of the power of the individual by that of the community is the decisive step toward civilization."

13   "Individual liberty is not an asset of civilization. It was greatest before there was any civilization, though admittedly even then it was largely worthless, because the individual was hardly in a position to defend it."

14   "It is almost as though the creation of a great human community would be most successful if there were no need for concern with individual happiness."

15   "All who wish to be more noble-minded than their constitution allows fall victim to neurosis; they would have been more healthy if it had been possible for them to be less good."

"Sublimation of the drives is a particularly striking feature of   16
cultural development, which makes it possible for the higher
mental activities – scientific, artistic and ideological – to play
such a significant role in civilized life."

"For a variety of reasons, I have no wish whatever to offer an   17
evaluation of human civilization. I have been careful to re-
frain from the enthusiastic prejudice that sees our civilization
as the most precious thing we possess or can acquire, and believes that its path will necessarily lead us to heights of perfection hitherto undreamt of."

"For there is a path that leads back from phantasy to reality –   18
the path, that is, of art."

"Substitutive satisfactions, such as art affords, are illusions   19
that contrast with reality, but they are not, for this reason,
any less effective psychically, thanks to the role that the ima-
gination has assumed in mental life."

"Modern literature is predominantly concerned with the   20
most questionable problems, which stir up all the passions,
and which encourage sensuality and a craving for pleasure,
and contempt for every fundamental ethical principle and
every ideal. It brings before the reader's mind pathological
figures, and problems concerned with psychopathic sexuality, revolution and other subjects."

21 "The plastic arts ... turn by preference to what is repellent, ugly and suggestive, and do not hesitate to set before our eyes with revolting fidelity the most horrible sights that reality has to offer."

22 *(on Salvador Dali)*
"For until then I was inclined to look upon surrealists, who have apparently chosen me for their patron saint, as absolute (let's say 95 percent, like alcohol) cranks. The young Spaniard, however, with his candid fanatical eyes and his undeniable technical mastery, has made me reconsider my opinion."

23 "An abstinent artist is hardly conceivable; but an abstinent young savant is certainly no rarity. The latter can, by his self-restraint, liberate forces for his studies; while the former probably finds his artistic achievements powerfully stimulated by his sexual experience."

24 "For I think you ought to know that in actual life I am terribly intolerant of cranks, that I see only the harmful side of them and that so far as these 'artists' are concerned I am almost one of those whom at the outset you castigate as philistines and lowbrows."

25 "Women stand for the interests of the family and sexual life, whereas the work of civilization has become more and more the business of the menfolk, setting them increasingly difficult tasks and obliging them to sublimate their drives – tasks for which women have little aptitude."

"... There are disproportionately more individuals hypo-critically simulating civilization than there are truly civilized people, indeed we might discuss the view that a certain degree of hypocritical pretence is indispensable for the maintenance of civilization, because the susceptibility to civilization of people living today might not be adequate to the task." 26

"Happiness is the belated fulfilment of a prehistoric wish. For this reason wealth brings so little happiness. Money was not a childhood wish." 27

"It is not the disease that is incurable, it is a man's social standing and his obligations that become an incurable disease." 28

"An officer is a miserable creature; he envies his equals, he bullies his subordinates, and is afraid of the higher-ups; the higher up he is himself, the more he is afraid." 29

"A great part of my life's work (I am ten years older than you) has been spent destroying illusions of my own and those of mankind. But if this one hope cannot be at least partly realized, if in the course of evolution we don't learn to divert our instincts from destroying our own kind, if we continue to hate one another for minor differences and kill each other for petty gain, if we go on exploiting the great progress made in the control of natural resources for our mutual destruction, what kind of future lies in store for us?" 30

31 "The communists think they have found the way to redeem mankind from evil. Man is unequivocally good and well disposed to his neighbour, but his nature has been corrupted by the institution of private property ... When private property is abolished, when goods are held in common and enjoyed by all, ill will and enmity among human beings will cease. Because all needs will be satisfied, no one will have any reason to see another person as his enemy; everyone will be glad to undertake whatever work is necessary ... I have no way of knowing whether the abolition of private property is expedient and beneficial. But I can recognize the psychological presumption behind it as a baseless illusion."

32 "When it comes to praise, one can take unlimited quantities, as anyone knows."

33 "As a rule, when I am attacked I can defend myself; but when I am praised, I am helpless."

34 "General impression: the world has acquired a certain respect for my work. But so far analysis has been accepted only by analysts."

35 "In the depths of my heart I can't help being convinced that my dear fellow men, with a few exceptions, are worthless."

36 "There is no mixture, however absurd, that society will not willingly swallow down if it is advertised as an antidote to the dreaded predominance of sexuality."

"Hysteria springs from the psychic constitution itself and is 37
an expression of the same organic basic power which produces the genius of an artist. But it is also a symptom of an especially strong and unresolved conflict which rages between
these basic tendencies and which later splits the psychic life
into two camps."

"Words were originally magic, and to this day words have 38
retained much of their ancient magical power. By words
one person can make another blissfully happy or drive him
to despair, by words the teacher conveys his knowledge to
his pupils, by words the orator carries his audience with him
and determines their judgements and decisions. Words pro-
voke affects and are in general the means of mutual influence
among men. Thus we shall not depreciate the use of words in
psychotherapy and we shall be pleased if we can listen to the
words that pass between the analyst and his patient."

"I simply cannot expose any more of my nakedness to the 39
reader …"

==

Sources

1   *Sexual Morality,* 1961, p. 186
2   *Civilization,* 2004, p. 37
3   *Civilization,* 2004, p. 65
4   *Civilization,* 2004, p. 38
5   *Civilization,* 2004, p. 36
6   *Civilization,* 2004, p. 39
7   *Civilization,* 2004, p. 39

8   *The Joke,* 2002, p. 98

9   *Civilization,* 2004, p. 45

10   *The Joke,* 2002, p. 123

11   *The Joke,* 2002, p. 38

12   *Civilization,* 2004, p. 41

13   *Civilization,* 2004, p. 42

14   *Civilization,* 2004, p. 99

15   *Sexual Morality,* 1961, p. 191

16   *Civilization,* 2004, p. 44

17   *Civilization,* 2004, p. 105

18   *Introductory Lectures,* 1961, p. 375 f.

19   *Civilization,* 2004, p. 15

20   *Sexual Morality,* 1961, p. 183 f.

21   *Sexual Morality,* 1961, p. 184

22   *Letters,* 1961, p. 449, 20 July 1938, to Stefan Zweig

23   *Sexual Morality,* 1961, p. 197

24   *Letters,* 1961, p. 331, 21 June 1920, to Oskar Pfister

25   *Civilization,* 2004, p. 51.

26   *War and Death,* 2005, p. 179

27   *Freud/Fliess,* 1985, p. 294, 16 Jan. 1898

28   *Letters,* 1961, p. 156, 25 June 1885, to Martha Bernays

29   *Letters,* 1961, p. 219, 1 Sept. 1886, to Josef Breuer

30   *Letters,* 1961, p. 341 f., 4 March 1923, to Romain Rolland

31   *Civilization,* 2004, p. 62 f.

32   *Letters,* 1961, p. 431, 8 Oct. 1936, to Ludwig Binswanger

33   *Letters,* 1961, p. 368, 10 May 1926, to Marie Bonaparte

34   *Letters,* 1961, p. 369, 10 May 1926, to Marie Bonaparte

35   *Letters,* 1961, p. 390, 28 July 1929, to Lou Andreas-Salomé

36   *Lay Analysis,* 1961, p. 187 f.

37   *Letters,* 1961, p. 332, 19 Oct. 1920, to Stefan Zweig

38   *Introductory Lectures,* 1961, p. 16

39   *Freud/Jung,* 1991, p. 216, 17 Feb. 1911

IV
CONFLICT AND STRIFE

"As long as the conditions of life of the various nations are so different and the conflicts between them so violent, wars will be inevitable."

Sigmund Freud addressed the theme of conflict in numerous writings. The most famous of these is the correspondence with Albert Einstein published as *Why War?* In response to an idea proposed by the League of Nations, Einstein wrote a letter to Freud in which he attempted to answer the question of the causes of military conflicts from his perspective and requested that Freud share his own views. The ensuing correspondence was published in book form in 1933. Before the backdrop of the rise of National Socialism and the privations of the First World War, Freud outlines a pessimistic worldview in his letter to Einstein. He writes of the inherent difficulties in fulfilling the postulate of altruism, and also discusses brute force, without which there can be no rule of law. This perspective can be traced through many of his publications, letters and lectures. Freud's assumptions seemed to be confirmed by the growing virulence of anti-Semitism – in his youth he had already suffered discrimination, and he well remembered his father's accounts of being subjected to insults.

Jewish students were treated badly at the University. Carl Koller, one of Freud's fellow students who later became a famous ophthalmologist, was even involved in a duel with another student who had insulted him and his Jewish heritage. Not only did Freud express his understanding: he actively approved of resorting to armed struggle as a response to anti-Semitism. Freud's Judaism stood in the way of a university career, as his early mentor Professor Ernst Brücke did not hesitate in telling him. In later years, Freud continued to voice his aggravation over this disappointment. He also saw the rejection to which he and his methods were subjected as having anti-Semitic undertones.

The hostility toward Jews reached its climax in the brutality of National Socialism. In 1933 Freud's writings were burned in Germany under the cry: "Against the soul-destroying glorification of instinctual life, for the nobility of the human soul!" After the *Anschluss* (the annexation of Austria by Nazi Germany) the Vienna Psychoanalytic Society disbanded, and almost all of its members fled into exile. Freud's four sisters, who were all living in Vienna at this time, were subsequently murdered in concentration camps. It was only thanks to his prominence and to the international connections of his friend Marie Bonaparte that Freud was able to flee.

In personal and professional relationships Freud could be quite combative, and he retained this energy to an advanced age. Capable of engaging both in passionate feuds and close friendships, he pursued his goals for the psychoanalytic movement with unbending determination. His correspondence with C. G. Jung, from which several of the following quotes originate, bears witness to Freud's toughness and calculating nature. Freud dumped Jung – who he had been close to for years as a fatherly friend and had courted as the "crown prince" of the psychoanalytic movement – when Jung began to develop his own psychological approach. Alfred Adler, another key figure in early psychoanalysis, fared no better when he left the tightly organized movement to pursue his own ideas: Freud dismissed his writings as "pathetic and vacuous". Freud could be venomous in his outrage over other people, as is demonstrated by the short quote concerning the German psychiatrist and sex researcher Albert Moll: "He had stunk up the room like the devil himself, and partly for lack of conviction and partly because he was my guest, I hadn't lambasted him enough."

Freud's relationship to his long-time mentor Josef Breuer was initially marked by deep affection. While Freud was still a student, Breuer, already a successful doctor, on occasion lent him money without ever demanding repayment. When Freud went into private practice, the internist referred many of his patients to the young nerve specialist. Together they wrote the 1895 book *Studies on Hysteria*, which would become a seminal work in the development of psychotherapy. Freud expressed his gratitude by naming his oldest daughter after Breuer's wife Mathilde. Selected quotes illustrate how Freud's relationship to Breuer cooled over the years and ended in rejection. After Breuer's death in 1925, Freud was polite and distanced in speaking of his earlier mentor. Both his admiration and his later antipathy for Breuer had faded.

Psychoanalysis endeavours to trace the origins of war, exploring ideas for countering armed conflict, if not preventing it. Sigmund Freud circumscribes the suppression of aggression in the sentence: "Everything that promotes the development of civilization also works against war." However, one must note that precisely the mastery of instincts subsumed under the concept of "civilization" can also lead to psychical disturbances, as is outlined in *Civilization and Its Discontents*. Seen before this background and with an awareness of his personal history, Freud's pessimistic view of human nature and his combative attitude are quite understandable. To a large degree, his standpoint derives from his lack of hope in the moral and peaceful behaviour of the human being.

=

"As long as the conditions of life of the various nations are so 1
different and the conflicts between them so violent, wars will
be inevitable."

"Men are strong so long as they represent a strong idea; they 2
become powerless when they oppose it."

" ... Love cannot be much younger than the lust to kill." 3

"*Homo homini lupus est.* Who, after all that he has learnt from 4
life and history, would be so bold as to dispute this propos-
ition?"

"At the very beginning, in a small horde of people, greater 5
muscle-power decided to whom something should belong,
or whose will should be enforced; the victor is the one with
the better weapons, or the one who uses them more skilfully.
With the introduction of weapons, intellectual superiority is
already beginning to assume the place of raw muscle-power."

6　"By making our enemy small, mean, contemptible, comical, we take a roundabout route to getting for ourselves the enjoyment of vanquishing him, which the third person – who has gone to no effort – endorses with his laughter."

7　"In childhood still endowed with powerful dispositions towards enmity, we later learn in the course of our more highly developed personal culture that it is unworthy to call people names; and even where a fight is actually permitted, the number of things that may not be employed as a means of carrying it on has increased markedly."

8　"With the abolition of private property the human love of aggression is robbed of one of its tools, a strong one no doubt, but certainly not the strongest."

9　"Even today, what our children learn as global history in school is essentially a sequence of genocides. The dark sense of guilt that has hung over humanity since primitive times, which in some religions has condensed into the hypothesis of an original sin, is probably the manifestation of a blood-guilt with which primitive man had burdened himself."

10　"The belligerent state permits itself any injustice, any violence that would disgrace the individual. It does not restrict itself to the accepted ruses, but also perpetrates calculated lies and deliberate treachery against the enemy, and to a degree that seems to exceed what was customary in earlier wars."

"We remember the old proverb: *Si vis pacem, para bellum*. If you wish to preserve peace, arm for war. This might be the time to alter it to read as follows: *Si vis vitam, para mortem*. If you wish to endure life, prepare yourself for death." 11

"Everything that promotes the development of civilization also works against war." 12

"Our little bit of civil war was not at all nice. You could not go out without your passport, electricity was cut off for a day, and the thought that the water supply might run out was very unpleasant. Now everything is calm, the calm of tension, you might say; just like waiting in a hotel room for the second shoe to be flung against the wall." 13

"In the case of war, Austria would be the next battlefield, and we are all lost. It is a poor consolation that I may not live to experience it, being that you would all remain." 14

"It is a part of the innate and ineradicable inequality of men that they divide into leaders and followers. The latter are the vast majority; they require an authority to make their decisions for them, and generally submit to that authority without question." 15

16   "It cannot go on like this; something is bound to happen. Whether the Nazis will come, or whether our home-made fascism will be ready in time, or whether Otto von Hapsburg will step in, as people now think."

17   "For where should I go in my state of dependence and physical helplessness? And everywhere abroad is so inhospitable. Only if there really were a satrap of Hitler's ruling in Vienna, I would no doubt have to go, no matter where. My attitude toward the parties who are quarrelling with one another I can only describe by plagiarising Shakespeare's Mercutio – 'A plague on both your houses.'"

18   "The future is uncertain; either Austrian fascism or the swastika. In the latter event we shall have to leave; native fascism we are willing to take in stride up to a certain point; it can hardly treat us as badly as its German cousin."

19   "We too of course are thankful for the bit of peace, but we cannot take any pleasure in it."

20   "Today we see law and violence as opposites. It is easy to demonstrate that the one has developed out of the other, and if we return to the very beginnings and check how it was that this first occurred, the solution of the problem presents itself to us without any difficulties ... Conflicts of interest between human beings are in principle resolved by the use of violence. That is how things are throughout the whole of the animal kingdom, from which man should not exclude himself."

"The individual is seldom inherently good or bad, being usu- 21
ally 'good' in one area, 'bad' in others. What is interesting is
the discovery that the pre-existence of strong 'bad' impulses
in childhood can often be seen as the actual pre-condition for
a distinct inclination towards 'good' in the adult. Those who
were most intensely egoistic in childhood can become the
most helpful and self-sacrificing citizens; most sentimental-
ists, humanitarians and protectors of animals have developed
out of little sadist and animal-tormentors."

"When I ask myself why I have always aspired to behave 22
honourably, to spare others and to be kind wherever possible,
and why I didn't cease doing so when I realized that in this
way one comes to harm and becomes an anvil, because other
people are brutal and unreliable, then indeed I have no answer."

"Some people are good simply because nothing bad enters 23
their heads, others are good because they manage – always
or frequently – to conquer their bad thoughts."

"I cannot be an optimist, and I believe I differ from the pess- 24
imists only insofar as wicked, stupid, senseless things don't
upset me, because I have accepted them from the beginning
as part of what the world is composed of."

"The rational explanation of heroism is based on the judge- 25
ment that one's own life cannot be as precious as certain abstract and universal possessions."

26　"'Dread' requires a specific object of which we are afraid. 'Fright', however, emphasizes the element of surprise; it describes the state that possesses us when we find ourselves plunged into danger without being prepared for it."

27　"I have already experienced in the resistance of the non-analyst what is now repeating itself in the resistance of the half-analyst."

28　"I have resigned myself to living like someone who speaks a foreign language or like Humboldt's parrot. Being the last of one's tribe – or the first and perhaps the only one – these are quite similar situations."

29　"It is good for the constitution to get things off one's chest."

30　"As long as I behave perfectly correctly, my worthy opponents are unsure. Only when I am doing exactly what they are doing will they feel certain that I am doing nothing better than they."

31　"I have long recognized that to stir up contradiction and arouse bitterness is the inevitable fate of psycho-analysis. I have come to the conclusion that I must be the true originator of all that is particularly characteristic in it."

32　"Experience shows that only very few people are capable of remaining polite – to say nothing of objective – in a scientific dispute. The impression made in me by scientific squabbles has always been odious."

"I am of course perfectly ready to allow that everyone has   33
a right to think and to write what he pleases; but he has no
right to put it forward as something other than what it really
is."

"It may be said lastly that by his 'modification' of psycho-ana-   34
lysis Jung has given us a counterpart to the famous Lichten-
berg knife. He has changed the hilt, and he has put a new
blade into it; yet because the same name is engraved on it,
we are expected to regard the instrument as the original one."

"Everything Adler has to say about dreams, the shibboleth of   35
psycho-analysis, is equally empty and unmeaning."

"An unwilling reviewer quickly turns into an odious one."   36

"The patients are disgusting and are giving me an opportun-   37
ity for new studies on technique. Eitingon is here and goes
for a walk with me twice a week after dinner, and has himself
analyzed at the same time."

(on Albert Moll)   38
"He had stunk up the room like the devil himself, and partly
for lack of conviction and partly because he was my guest, I
hadn't lambasted him enough."

"Breuer has again behaved splendidly in the Fleischl affair.   39
By saying only good things about him one doesn't give a
proper picture of his character; one ought to emphasize the
absence of so many bad things."

40   "Recently Breuer pulled another brilliant stunt. I would think that one should not let his intelligence deceive one about his narrow-mindedness."

41   *(on Breuer)*
"With all his great intellectual gifts, there was nothing Faustian in his nature."

42   *(on Karl Kraus)*
"If you are interested in other matters as well, the article in *Die Fackel* is probably only the precursor of other, more vigorous attacks; that is the way he always does it. He is a completely unreliable, malicious person."

43   "A human being must be able to pull himself together to form a judgement ..."

44   "One really must try not to become as wicked as people make one out, but one should learn to be careful."

45   "I always comfort myself with the fact that people subordinate to or on par with me have never considered me unpleasant, only superiors or people otherwise above me."

46   "Envy often spoils the enjoyment of gardens and country houses."

=

Sources

1 *War and Death,* 2005, p. 193

2 *History of the Movement,* 1961, p. 66

3 *War and Death,* 2005, p. 187

4 *Civilization,* 2004, p. 61

5 *Why War?,* 2005, p. 222

6 *The Joke,* 2002, p. 100

7 *The Joke,* 2002, p. 100

8 *Civilization,* 2004, p. 63

9 *War and Death,* 2005, p. 186

10 *War and Death,* 2005, p. 173

11 *War and Death,* 2005, p. 194

12 *Why War?,* 2005, p. 232

13 *Freud/Zweig,* 1970, p. 65, 25 Feb. 1934

14 *Briefe an die Kinder,* 2010, p. 432, 6 June 1934, to Ernst Freud

15 *Why War?,* 2005, p. 230

16 *Freud/Zweig,* 1970, p. 65, 25 Feb. 1934

17 *Freud/Zweig,* 1970, p. 65, 25 Feb. 1934

18 *Letters,* 1961, p. 420, 20 Feb. 1934, to Ernst Freud

19 *Letters,* 1961, p. 452, 4 Oct. 1938, to Marie Bonaparte

20 *Why War?,* 2005, p. 222

21 *War and Death,* 2005, p. 176

22 *Letters,* 1961, p. 308, 8 July 1915, to James J. Putnam

23 *Letters,* 1961, p. 198, 27 Jan. 1886, to Martha Bernays

24 *Letters,* 1961, p. 312, 30 July 1915, to Lou Andreas-Salomé

25 *War and Death,* 2005, p. 190

26 *Pleasure Principle,* 2003, p. 51

27 *Letters,* 1961, p. 299, 1 Jan. 1913, to James J. Putnam

28 *Freud/Fliess,* 1985, p. 430, 25 Nov. 1900

29 *Freud/Fliess,* 1985, p. 368, 27 Aug. 1899

30 *Freud/Fliess,* 1985, p. 408, 4 Apr. 1900

31 *History of the Movement,* 1961, p. 8

32 *History of the Movement,* 1961, p. 39

33 *History of the Movement,* 1961, p. 60 f.

34 *History of the Movement,* 1961, p. 66

35 *History of the Movement,* 1961, p. 57

36 *Freud/Fliess,* 1985, p. 408, 4 Apr. 1900

37 *Freud/Ferenczi,* 1993, p. 85, 22 Oct. 1909

38 *Freud/Jung,* p. 148, 16 May 1909

39 *Letters,* 1961, p. 149, 6 June 1885, to Martha Bernays

40 *Freud/Fliess,* 1985, p. 294, 16 Jan. 1898

41 *Letters,* 1961, p. 413, 2 June 1932, to Arnold Zweig

42 *Briefe an die Kinder,* 2010, p. 64, 12 June 1908, to Mathilde Freud

43 *Letters,* 1961, p. 160, 5 July 1885, to Martha Bernays

44 *Letters,* 1961, p. 201, 2 Feb. 1886, to Martha Bernays

45 *Letters,* 1961, p. 202, 2 Feb. 1886, to Martha Bernays

46 *Letters,* 1961, p. 249, 17 Sept. 1905, to Alexander Freud

V

DREAM AND ILLUSION

"Dreams are never concerned with trivialities;
we do not allow our sleep to be disturbed
by trifles."

After completing his studies, Sigmund Freud established himself as a neuropathologist in private practice. With the publication in 1895 of *Studies on Hysteria* (written together with Josef Breuer), Freud became a topic of discussion in medical circles. In 1899 he completed *The Interpretation of Dreams*, which in historical and literary terms represents the definitive inception of psychoanalysis.

Freud understands the dream as a vehicle for comprehending psychical processes: it is a result of the past and in no way a glimpse of the future. He noted that this approach was by no means new, citing thinkers of antiquity such as Plato, who considered the dream to be a source of self-knowledge and attributed therapeutic effects to its messages.

In addition to being the first written statement of psychoanalytic dream theory, *The Interpretation of Dreams* achieved fame for its uncompromising openness in revealing details of Freud's innermost self – to this day readers remain fascinated by this aspect. Freud analyzes many of his own dreams, revealing his fears, his childhood memories and the burdens of his everyday life. Despite his censorship of several dreams and their analyses to protect his private sphere, Freud discloses deeply personal issues and perspectives. In the tradition of the medical self-experiment, he presents himself, his dreams and their interpretations as his object of study.

Freud's biographers Ernest Jones and Peter Gay see the significance of this work for Freud himself in his comprehensive self-analysis. The authors speculate that Freud was not only protecting himself by omitting details from his dreams, but that he also unconsciously withheld various elements. Peter Gay writes: "Freud's *Interpretation of Dreams* is about more than dreams. It is an autobiography at once candid and canny, as tantalizing in what it omits as in what it discloses." The book was also of great methodological importance in the development of psychoanalysis: it contains precise directions for analyzing dreams, and thus it is a historic landmark as the first text to set down details of psychoanalytic technique.

The book grew with every edition, as Freud and his colleagues updated and reworked it, adding commentaries and new sections. In later editions, case histories contributed by other analysts were also included, and thus the book remained up to date with the continuing development of psychoanalytic theory, while the breadth and density of its exemplary material grew. This speaks for the work's pivotal significance, as does Freud's characterization of dream interpretation toward the end of the book as "the royal road to a knowledge of the unconscious activities of the mind." In his book on dreams and dream interpretation, Wolfgang Mertens writes: "Freud was the first to prove, through the continual analysis of his own dreams, that the seemingly meaningless and puzzling images of dreams bring to light repressed psychical material that can be integrated sensibly into the realm of meaningful thought."

Freud's key postulate of dream interpretation is that of wish fulfilment: the dreamer's unconscious desires and interests are fulfilled in the dream. This can occur directly and

77

with hardly any dissimulation, or in a distorted transformation requiring interpretation. Freud attempted to resolve this distortion by separating the dream's manifest and latent content. Manifest content comprises the events of the dream as they are remembered. Latent content is concealed behind the dream's manifest content and must be decoded. Through the "dream-work" the latent content of the dream is made manifest, whereby it is "censored". This censorship involves a variety of processes, such as condensation (multiple meanings are brought together in a single person or object) and displacement (the meaning of a person, object or action is attributed to a different person, object or action). "Considerations of representability" must also be taken into account: dreams represent thoughts and abstract ideas as concrete images. A temporal sequence of events suggests a cause-and-effect relationship; since the dream is not in a position to express a negation visually, it is expressed by representing people and events through their opposites. Thus the images of the dream are not simply what they appear to be: they are vestiges of psychical activity that can be traced by analyzing the relationships between the images.

For this purpose, psychoanalysis makes use of the technique of "free association". The psychoanalyst uses this technique to recognize each individual's characteristic censorship methods and the varying meanings that representations can have for him or her, which is particularly useful in decoding dreams. The most well-known element of censorship is the use of symbols, especially to encode sexual content. Freud's method of interpretation caused quite a stir, and the controversy surrounding it may well have contributed to the growing commercial success enjoyed by *The Interpretation of Dreams* over the years. Today one can hardly imagine being shocked at the idea that a dreamed candle, snake or column could stand for a phallus, broken teeth for castration, or scrubbing movements for masturbation – at the turn of the century, these ideas were bound to encounter considerable resistance.

====

"Dreams are never concerned with trivialities; we do not allow our sleep to be disturbed by trifles." 1

"The interpretation of dreams is the royal road to a knowledge of the unconscious activities of the mind." 2

"Interpreting dreams appears to be more difficult for others than I had indicated." 3

"The study of dreams may be regarded as the most reliable approach route for those seeking to understand the deep-level processes of the psyche." 4

"We find our way to the understanding ('interpretation') of a dream by assuming that what we recollect as the dream after we have woken up is not the true dream-process but only a facade behind which that process lies concealed." 5

6   "This formula suggests itself to me: What is *seen* in the pre-
    historic period produces dreams; what is *heard* in it produces
    phantasies; what is *experienced sexually* in it produces psy-
    choneuroses."

7   "For the Greeks and other oriental nations, there may have
    been times when a campaign without dream-interpreters
    seemed as impossible as one without air-reconnaissance
    seems today."

8   "I think, however, that the Roman emperor was in the wrong
    when he had one of his subjects executed because he had
    dreamt of murdering the emperor. He should have begun by
    trying to find out what the dream meant; most probably its
    meaning was not what it had appeared to be."

9   "And the value of dreams for giving us knowledge of the fu-
    ture? There is of course no question of that. It would be truer
    to say that they give us knowledge of the past. For dreams
    are derived from the past in every sense."

10 "Not only dreams are wish fulfilments, so are hysterical at-
    tacks."

11 "When the work of interpretation has been completed, we
    perceive that a dream is the fulfilment of a wish."

"It will be noticed how conveniently everything was arranged in this dream. Since its only purpose was to fulfil a wish, it could be completely egotistical." 12

"I do not myself know what animals dream of. But a proverb, 13 to which my attention was drawn by one of my students, does claim to know. 'What,' asks the proverb, 'do geese dream of?' And it replies: 'Of maize.' The whole theory that dreams are wish-fulfilments is contained in these two phrases."

"All dreams are in a sense dreams of convenience. They 14 serve the purpose of prolonging sleep instead of waking up. Dreams are the guardians of sleep and not its disturbers."

"Dreams, as everyone knows, may be confused, unintelligible or positively nonsensical. What they say may contradict all that we know of reality, and we behave in them like insane people, since, so long we are dreaming, we attribute objective reality to the contents of the dream." 15

"Not only does the dream have no need to place any value on 16 intelligibility, it must even guard against being understood, for otherwise it would be destroyed; it can only exist in disguise."

"The dream predominantly serves to spare ourselves un- 17 pleasure, the joke to gain pleasure; but in these two aims, all our psychical activities meet."

18 "The restoration of the connections which the dream-work has destroyed is a task which has to be performed by the interpretative process."

19 "Transformation of dream-thoughts so that they become representable, condensation and displacement are the three major functions we may ascribe to the dream-work."

20 "Since we have learned to understand even mad and confused dreams, we know that every time we go to sleep we cast aside our hard-earned morality, acquired as though it were a piece of clothing, to put it back on again in the morning. This baring of ourselves is, of course, not dangerous, because we pose no threat, being paralysed by the sleeping state and condemned to inactivity … Thus, for example, it is noteworthy that all our dreams are governed by purely selfish motives."

21 "Representation by the opposite is so common in dreams that even popular, quite mistaken, books of dream-interpretation habitually reckon with it."

22 "Dreams are brief, meagre and laconic in comparison with the range and wealth of the dream-thoughts."

23 "Dreams are only a form of thinking; one can never reach an understanding of this form by reference to the content of the thoughts; only an appreciation of the dream-work will lead to that understanding."

"It is perfectly true that dreams contain symbolizations of 24 bodily organs and functions, that water in a dream often points to a urinary stimulus, and that the male genitals can be represented by an upright stick or a pillar, and so on."

"Boxes, cases, chests, cupboards and ovens represent the 25 uterus, and also hollow objects, ships, and vessels of all kind."

"In men's dreams a necktie often appears as a symbol for the 26 penis. No doubt this is not only because neckties are long, dependent objects and peculiar to men, but also because they can be chosen according to taste – a liberty, which, in the case of the object symbolized, is forbidden by Nature."

"To represent castration symbolically, the dream-work makes 27 use of baldness, hair-cutting, falling out of teeth and decapitation. If one of the ordinary symbols for a penis occurs in a dream doubled or multiplied, it is to be regarded as a warding-off of castration."

"Dreams of being naked or insufficiently dressed in the pres- 28 ence of strangers sometimes occur with the additional feature of there being a complete absence of any such feeling as shame on the dreamer's part. We are only concerned here, however, with those dreams of being naked in which one *does* feel shame and embarrassment and tries to escape or hide, and is then overcome by a strange inhibition which prevents one from moving and makes one feel incapable of altering one's distressing situation."

29   "Children in dreams often stand for the genitals; and, indeed, both men and women are in the habit of referring to their genitals affectionately as their 'little ones'."

30   "Today, just as then, many men dream of having sexual relations with their mothers, and speak of the fact with indignation and astonishment."

31   "Dreams, then, are often most profound when they seem most crazy. In every epoch of history, those who have had something to say but could not say it without peril have eagerly assumed a fool's cap."

32   "The question whether it is possible to interpret every dream must be answered in the negative. It must not be forgotten that in interpreting a dream we are opposed by the psychical forces which were responsible for its distortion."

33   "A dream, then, is a psychosis, with all the absurdities, delusions and illusions of a psychosis. A psychosis of short duration, no doubt, harmless, even entrusted with a useful function, introduced with the subject's consent and terminated by an act of his will."

34   "The whole plea – for the dream was nothing else – reminded one vividly of the defence put forward by the man who was charged by one of his neighbours with having given him back a borrowed kettle in a damaged condition. The defendant asserted first, that he had given it back undamaged; secondly, that the kettle had a hole in it when he borrowed

it; and thirdly, that he had never borrowed a kettle from his neighbour at all."

"The misinterpretation is not an illusion but, as one might say, an evasion." 35

"The life imposed on us is too hard for us to bear: it brings 36 too much pain, too many disappointments, too many insoluble problems. If we are to endure it, we cannot do without palliative measures. Of such measures there are perhaps three kinds: powerful distractions, which cause us to make light of our misery, substitutive satisfactions, which diminish it, and intoxicants, which anaesthetize us to it."

"The effect of intoxicants in the struggle for happiness and in 37 keeping misery at a distance is seen as so great a boon that not only individuals, but whole nations, have accorded them a firm place in the economy of the libido. We owe to them not only a direct yield of pleasure, but also a fervently desired degree of independence from the external world. We know, after all, that by 'drowning our sorrows' we can escape at any time from the pressure of reality and find refuge in a world of our own that affords us better conditions for our sensibility."

"Bearing life is, after all, the first duty of all living beings. 38 The illusion loses its value if it hinders us in that."

39 "I need say little about the interpretation of dreams. It came as the first fruits of the technical innovation I had adopted when, following a dim presentiment, I decided to replace hypnosis by free association."

40 "The interpretation of dreams became a solace and a support to me in those arduous first years of analysis, when I had to master the technique, clinical phenomena and therapy of the neuroses all at the same time. During that period I was completely isolated, and in the network of problems and accumulation of difficulty I often dreaded losing my bearings and also my confidence."

41 "Somewhere inside me there is a feeling for form, an appreciation of beauty as a kind of perfection; and the tortuous sentences of my dream book, with their parading of indirect phrases and squinting at ideas, deeply offend one of my ideals."

42 "Whether or not people like the dream book is beginning to leave me cold and I am beginning to bemoan its fate. This one drop has obviously not made the stone any softer."

43 "The 'silence of the forest' is the clamour of a metropolis compared to the silence in my consulting room. This is a good place to 'dream'."

"Do you suppose that someday one will read on a marble tab-
let on this house: 'Here, on July 24, 1895, the secret of the
dream revealed itself to Dr. Sigm. Freud.' So far there is little
prospect of it."

=

SOURCES

1   *Dreams*, 1961, p. 182
2   *Dreams*, 1961, p. 608
3   *Freud/Fliess*, 1985, p. 389, 26 Nov. 1899
4   *Pleasure Principle*, 2003, p. 51
5   *An Outline of Psycho-Analysis*, 1961, p. 165
6   *Freud/Fliess*, 1985, p. 302, 10 March 1898
7   *Introductory Lectures*, 1961, p. 85 f.
8   *Dreams*, 1961, p. 620
9   *Dreams*, 1961, p. 621
10 *Freud/Fliess*, 1985, p. 345, 19 Feb. 1899
11 *Dreams*, 1961, p. 121
12 *Dreams*, 1961, p. 124
13 *Dreams*, 1961, p. 132
14 *Dreams*, 1961, p. 233
15 *An Outline of Psycho-Analysis*, 1961, p. 165
16 *The Joke*, 2002, p. 174f.
17 *The Joke*, 2002, p. 175
18 *Dreams*, 1961, p. 312
19 *The Joke*, 2002, p. 161
20 *War and Death*, 2005, p. 180
21 *The Joke*, 2002, p. 77
22 *Dreams*, 1961, p. 279
23 *History of the Movement*, 1961, p. 65
24 *Dreams*, 1961, p. 227
25 *Dreams*, 1961, p. 354
26 *Dreams*, 1961, p. 356

27 *Dreams,* 1961, p. 357

28 *Dreams,* 1961, p. 242

29 *Dreams,* 1961, p. 357

30 *Dreams,* 1961, p. 364

31 *Dreams,* 1961, p. 444

32 *Dreams,* 1961, p. 524 f.

33 *An Outline of Psycho-Analysis,* 1961, p. 172

34 *Dreams,* 1961, p. 119 f.

35 *Dreams,* 1961, p. 235

36 *The Joke,* 2002, p. 14 f.

37 *Civilization,* 2004, p. 19

38 *War and Death,* 2005, p. 193 f.

39 *History of the Movement,* 1961, p. 19

40 *History of the Movement,* 1961, p. 20

41 *Freud/Fliess,* 1985, p. 373 f., 21 Sept. 1899

42 *Freud/Fliess,* 1985, p. 422, 10 July 1900

43 *Freud/Fliess,* 1985, p. 354, 9 June 1899

44 *Freud/Fliess,* 1985, p. 417, 12 June 1900

VI

EROS AND SEXUALITY

"'Beauty' and 'attractiveness' are originally properties of the sexual object. It is notable that the genitals themselves, the sight of which is always exciting, are hardly ever judged beautiful; on the other hand, the quality of beauty seems to attach to certain secondary sexual characteristics."

E ros and sexuality occupy a central position in the work of Sigmund Freud. Taking the idea of sexuality as a point of departure, Freud's analyses went far beyond any conventional narrow definitions, approaching philosophical conceptions of Eros, cultural sexual morality and sexual deviation. Freud recognized the life drive – Eros – as the first and main instinct of human life, and he linked it to self-preservation and the preservation of the species, survival and procreation. He saw the libido as the vital psychical energy of the life drive, which seeks pleasure from the self and others as well as from nonhuman objects. (In psychoanalytic terminology, the word *object* almost always refers to a *person* toward whom action or desire is directed.) To describe the focusing of the libido on an object, Freud introduced the concept of *Besetzung*. In a psychological context, this everyday German word means the "investment" of psychical energy in an (external) object. For the English versions of his work, Freud's translators invented the neologism *cathexis* to translate *Besetzung*. Here, as in many cases, the translators' turn to Greek (or Latin) has lent Freud's work an air of esotericism that it lacks in the original German. Within the framework of this "economy of the libido", Freud was convinced that inhibition of the sex drive can have grave consequences: "In addition to all those who are homosexuals by virtue of their organization, or who became so in their childhood, there must be reckoned the great number of those in whom, in their maturer years, a blocking of the main stream of their libido has caused a widening in the side-channel of homosexuality."

Freud drew key insights regarding the life and death drives – Eros and Thanatos – by comparing and contrasting their individual aspects. Eros generally stands for love and sexual desire. We yearn to unite ourselves with the other. However, this desire to merge into the other is also linked to the danger of destroying the object. Thus the objects that we love and desire are also the ones that we want to destroy. The life drive Eros aims to develop bonds with others, while Thanatos, the death drive, strives to dissolve objects. If a drive is not bound by a moderating psychical agency, either pure destructive rage or pure happiness break through.

In exploring this widely branched complex of themes, Freud pursued two different strategies, which often produced contradictory results. As a physician he focused on the problem by posing strictly scientific questions and by making reference to verified biological and physiological knowledge. As a psychoanalyst, on the other hand, his interest was oriented toward the determining psychical factors of sexuality, whose influence on the psychical development of the individual begins in infancy. Thus Freudian theory puts infantile sexuality, i. e. human sexuality from birth until the beginning of puberty, at the centre of interest. Beyond normal sexual development, neurotic or perverse deviations are also seen as being rooted in this period. Freud maintains that the workings of sexuality can already be observed in the newborn baby. As the child grows, it displays sexual impulses that develop from the initial oral phase through the anal and phallic phases. Reaching its highpoint around age four, infantile sexuality is then increasingly suppressed in the following period of latency. Sexual energy is undirected in infants and toddlers: initially it is discharged indiscriminately, whereby the child's action is steered by the pleasure principle alone. At this age, the drives are only directed toward feelings of pleasure, which arise through the satisfaction of desires. It is not until the advent of puberty that they are laden with new intensity, giving rise to the inner conflicts of adult life, particularly in view of the increasing demands of the reality principle. Freud describes the functioning of the drives as a dynamic flow of psychical energy between the three agencies of the psyche: the id, the ego and the super-ego.

Even in the sexual behaviour of adults, Freud believed that in a psychoanalytic sense he could prove the continued workings of the sexual inhibitions and disturbances of early childhood. The somatic aspects of sexuality faded into the background. His theories also reflect a decadent epoch, which in the shadows of an opulently staged lifestyle had long since begun to free itself from rigid sexual morality. In this respect, Freud's 1908 essay "'Civilized' Sexual Morality and Modern Nervous Illness" is of particular importance as a revealing overview of current sexual morality and sexual practice. It is rooted in the research findings that also went into the landmark 1905 publication *Three Essays on the Theory of Sexuality*. In both works, Freud illuminates how society demands the sublimation of the individual's sexual energies and discusses the resulting difficulties for the individual. According to Freud, these demands do great harm to the sexual life of the human being in civilization. The permanent, indissoluble bonding of the man to the woman in marriage cannot satisfy male sexuality. And yet, on account of the era's double moral standards, this readily apparent impasse continued to go unmentioned, Freud summarized resignedly. Thus he also engaged in a critical exploration of alternate sources of satisfaction, such as masturbation, whereby he at times chose to take a humorous approach to explaining his ideas; for example, by quoting Karl Kraus's dictum: "Copulation is no more than an unsatisfying substitute for masturbation." The dirty joke, on the other hand, revealed to him the teller's hidden proclivity toward exhibitionism ...

Many of Freud's ideas were based on his theory of drives, according to which every drive seeks out its own aim or object. The source of the drive, in Freudian thinking, is that which is able to awaken or trigger it. Freud's examples range from the satisfaction of desires in early childhood, such as sucking the mother's breast or the thumb, to the sex drive. Here he observed that desires or deprivations often continue to exist in the unconscious, expressing themselves in later life through undefinable restlessness, irritability or frustration.

=

" 'Beauty' and 'attractiveness' are originally properties of the 1
sexual object. It is notable that the genitals themselves, the sight of which is always exciting, are hardly ever judged beautiful; on the other hand, the quality of beauty seems to attach to certain secondary sexual characteristics."

"A pity that one always keeps one's mouth shut about the 2
most intimate things."

3   "At the height of erotic passion the borderline between ego and object is in danger of becoming blurred."

4   "We never have so little protection against suffering as when we are in love; we are never so desolate as when we have lost the object of our love or its love for us."

5   "When a love relationship is at its height, the lovers no longer have any interest in the world around them; they are self-sufficient as a pair, and in order to be happy they do not even need the child they have in common."

6   "If I love another person, he must in some way deserve it … He deserves it if, in certain important respects, he so much resembles me that in him I can love myself. He deserves it if he is so much more perfect than myself that in him I can love an ideal image of myself."

7   "That is how exclusive I am when I love."

8   "How bold one gets when one is sure of being loved!"

9   "There is something terrible about two human beings who love each other and can find neither the means nor the time to let the other know, who wait until some misfortune or disagreement extorts an affirmation of affection."

10   "Why don't we get drunk? Because the discomfort and disgrace of the after-effects gives us more 'unpleasure' than

the pleasure we derive from getting drunk. Why don't we fall in love with a different person every month? Because at each separation a part of our heart would be torn away. Why don't we make a friend of everyone? Because the loss of him or any misfortune befalling him would affect us deeply."

"Don't you feel rather proud of being able to make someone so far away so happy?" 11

"One can love one another properly only when one is close. What is a memory compared to what one can behold!" 12

"Darling, is it possible that you can be affectionate only in summer and that in winter you freeze up? Now sit down and answer me at once so that I will still have time to get myself a winter girl." 13

"It is very strange to watch one's little daughter *(Sophie Freud)* suddenly turn into a loving woman." 14

"Maybe you know already that love must be learned just like everything else. Thus it is hard to avoid making mistakes; it doesn't have to be the first love that becomes the lasting one." 15

"That marriage is not an institution that satisfies the husband's sexuality is something one is not bold enough to say loud and in public …" 16

17 "Fear of the consequences of sexual intercourse first brings the married couple's physical affection to an end; and then, as a remoter result, it usually puts a stop as well to the mental sympathy between them, which should have been the successor to their original passionate love. The spiritual disillusionment and bodily deprivation to which most marriages are thus doomed puts both partners back in the state they were in before their marriage, except for being the poorer by the loss of an illusion, and they must once more have recourse to their fortitude in mastering and deflecting their sexual instinct."

18 "Two things might give rise to a feeling of anxiety in *coitus interruptus*: in the woman, the fear of becoming pregnant; in the man, worry of failing at the trick."

19 "I have found, in my own case too, the phenomenon of being in love with my mother and jealous of my father, and now I consider it a universal event in early childhood, even if not so early as in children who have been made hysterical."

20 "In my opinion it is advisable in general, and quite especially where neurotics are concerned, to assume the existence of the complete Oedipus complex."

21 "Sexual morality as defined by society, in its most extreme form that of America, strikes me as very contemptible. I stand for an infinitely freer sexual life, although I myself have made very little use of such freedom. Only so far as I considered myself entitled to."

"After all, the sexual life of civilized man has been seriously 22 damaged; at times one has the impression that as a function it is subject to a process of involution, such as our teeth and our hair seem to be undergoing as organs."

"The 'double' sexual morality which is valid for men in our 23 society is the plainest admission that society itself does not believe in the possibility of enforcing the precepts which it itself has laid down."

"If a man is energetic in winning the object of his love, we are 24 confident that he will pursue his other aims with an equally unswerving energy; but if, for all sorts of reasons, he refrains from satisfying his strong sexual instincts, his behaviour will be conciliatory and resigned rather than vigorous in other spheres of life as well."

"There are two kinds of women patients: one kind who are as 25 loyal to their doctor as to their husband, and the other kind who change their doctors as often as their lovers."

"The inclination to gaze on what is specific to each sex in its 26 nakedness is one of the original components of our libido."

"Anyone who laughs at the bawdy talk they have heard is 27 laughing like a spectator at an act of sexual aggression."

"After all, sadism was clearly part of sexual life, in which 28 cruelty could replace tenderness."

29   "In young children it is easy to observe the inclination to show themselves naked."

30   "In childhood the female genitals and the anus are regarded as a single area – the 'bottom' (in accordance with the infantile 'cloaca theory'). It is not until later that the discovery is made that this region of the body comprises two separate cavities and orifices."

31   "Sexual life does not begin only at puberty, but starts with plain manifestations soon after birth."

32   "The first organ to emerge as an erotogenic zone and to make libidinal demands on the mind is, from the time of birth onwards, the mouth."

33   "The baby's obstinate persistence in sucking gives evidence at an early stage of a need for satisfaction which, though it originates from and is instigated by the taking of nourishment, nevertheless strives to obtain pleasure independently of nourishment, and for that reason may and should be termed *sexual*."

34   "Analysis very often shows that a little girl, after she has had to relinquish her father as a love-object, will bring her masculinity into prominence and identify herself with her father (that is, with the object which has been lost), instead of with her mother. This will clearly depend on whether the masculinity in her disposition – whatever that may consist in – is strong enough."

"Quite frequently a brother is a sexual pervert, while his sister, who, being a women, possesses a weaker sexual instinct, is a neurotic whose symptoms express the same inclinations as the perversions of her sexually more active brother. And correspondingly, in many families the men are healthy, but from a social point of view immoral to an undesirable degree, while the women are high-minded and over-refined, but severely neurotic." 35

"As we have discovered, the symptoms of neuroses are essentially substitutive satisfactions for unfulfilled sexual desires." 36

"If one questioned a young patient as to whether he has ever masturbated, the only answer one would get would be: 'O na, nie' *(lit: 'Oh no, never'; Onanie: 'masturbation').*" 37

"The insight has dawned on me that masturbation is the one major habit, the 'primary addiction', and it is only as a substitute and replacement for it that the other addictions – to alcohol, morphine, tobacco, and the like – come into existence." 38

"Many people who boast of succeeding in being abstinent have only been able to do so with the help of masturbation and similar satisfactions which are linked with the autoerotic sexual activities of early childhood." 39

40   "Masturbation ... is far from meeting the ideal demands of civilized sexual morality, and consequently drives young people into the same conflicts with the ideals of education which they hoped to escape by abstinence. Furthermore, it vitiates the character through indulgence, and this in more than one way. In the first place, it teaches people to achieve important aims without taking trouble and by easy paths instead of through an energetic exertion of force – that is, it follows the principle that sexuality lays down the pattern of behaviour; secondly, in the phantasies that accompany satisfaction the sexual object is raised to a degree of excellence which is not easily found again in reality. A witty writer (Karl Kraus in the Vienna paper *Die Fackel*) once expressed this truth in reverse by cynically remarking: 'Copulation is no more than an unsatisfying substitute for masturbation.'"

41   "In addition to all those who are homosexuals by virtue of their organization, or who became so in their childhood, there must be reckoned the great number of those in whom, in their maturer years, a blocking of the main stream of their libido has caused a widening in the side-channel of homosexuality."

42   "It is a great injustice to persecute homosexuality as a crime, and a cruelty, too."

43   "According to our hypothesis, man's drives are of two kinds only: those which seek to preserve and unite – we call them erotic, exactly in the sense in which Plato uses the word Eros in his *Symposium*, or sexual, with a deliberate over-extension

of the popular conception of sexuality – and others which see to destroy and kill – we sum these up as the drive to aggression or the drive to destruction ... Each one of these drives is just as essential as the other, and the manifestations of life arise out of the concurrent and mutually opposing effects of each."

"Human beings have made such strides in controlling the forces of nature that, with the help of these forces, they will have no difficulty in exterminating one another, down to the last man. They know this, and it is this knowledge that accounts for much of their present disquiet, unhappiness and anxiety. And now it is to be expected that the other of the two 'heavenly powers', immortal Eros, will try to assert himself in the struggle with his equally immortal adversary." 44

"The ejection of the sexual substances in the sexual act corresponds in a sense to the separation of soma and germplasms. This accounts for the likeness of the condition that follows complete sexual satisfaction to dying, and for the fact that death coincides with the act of copulation in some of the lower animals." 45

"In the sexual processes we have the indispensable 'organic foundation' without which a medical man can only feel ill at ease in the life of the psyche." 46

"In the meantime things have become more lively. The sexual business attracts people who are all stunned and then go away 47 won over after having exclaimed, 'No one has ever asked me about that before!'"

48 "We are being asked neither more nor less than to abjure our belief in the sexual drive. The only answer is to profess it openly …"

=

Sources

1 *Civilization,* 2004, p. 25 f.
2 *Freud/Fliess,* 1985, p. 285, 3 Dec. 1897
3 *Civilization,* 2004, p. 3
4 *Civilization,* 2004, p. 25
5 *Civilization,* 2004, p. 56
6 *Civilization,* 2004, p. 58
7 *Letters,* 1961, p. 9, 19 June 1882, to Martha Bernays
8 *Letters,* 1961, p. 11, 27 June 1882, to Martha Bernays
9 *Letters,* 1961, p. 27 f., 18 Aug. 1882, to Martha Bernays
10 *Letters,* 1961, p. 50, 29 Aug. 1883, to Martha Bernays
11 *Letters,* 1961, p. 94, 28 Jan. 1884, to Martha Bernays
12 *Letters,* 1961, p. 158, 26 June 1885, to Martha Bernays
13 *Letters,* 1961, p. 136, 21 Jan. 1885, to Martha Bernays
14 *Letters,* 1961, p. 290, 24 July 1912, to Max Halberstadt
15 *Briefe an die Kinder,* 2010, p. 56, 6 May 1908, to Mathilde Freud
16 *The Joke,* 2002, p.108
17 *Sexual Morality,* 1961, p. 194 f.
18 *Freud/Fliess,* 1985, p. 78, 21 May 1894
19 *Freud/Fliess,* 1985, p. 272, 15 Oct. 1897
20 *The Ego and the Id,* 1961, p. 32
21 *Letters,* 1961, p. 308, 8 July 1915, to James J. Putnam
22 *Civilization,* 2004, p. 53
23 *Sexual Morality,* 1961, p. 195
24 *Sexual Morality,* 1961, p. 198

25 *Freud/Fliess*, 1985, p. 110, 24 Jan. 1895

26 *The Joke*, 2002, p. 95

27 *The Joke*, 2002, p. 95

28 *Civilization*, 2004, p. 69

29 *The Joke*, 2002, p. 95

30 *Dreams*, 1961, p. 354 f.

31 *An Outline of Psycho-Analysis*, 1961, p. 152

32 *An Outline of Psycho-Analysis*, 1961, p. 153

33 *An Outline of Psycho-Analysis*, 1961, p. 154

34 *The Ego and the Id*, 1961, p. 32

35 *Sexual Morality*, 1961, p. 191 f.

36 *Civilization*, 2004, p. 97

37 *The Joke*, 2002, p. 25

38 *Freud/Fliess*, 1985, p. 287, 22 Dec. 1897

39 *Sexual Morality*, 1961, p. 199

40 *Sexual Morality*, 1961, p. 199 f.

41 *Sexual Morality*, 1961, p. 200 f.

42 *Briefe*, 1968, p. 438, 9 April 1935, to N. N.

43 *Why War?*, 2005, p. 227

44 *Civilization*, 2004, p. 106

45 *The Ego and the Id*, 1961, p. 47

46 *Freud/Jung*, 1991, p. 108, 19 April 1908

47 *Freud/Fliess*, 1985, p. 57, 6 Oct. 1893

48 *Freud/Jung*, 1991, p. 58, 7 April 1907

VII

SCIENCE AND ANALYSIS

"It is not easy
to treat feelings scientifically."

In founding psychoanalysis, Sigmund Freud created a new form of therapy for psychological problems. At the same time, he saw his creation as an innovative science. Thus he set out to create a theoretical superstructure formulating his new psychical research into an independent school of thought with major implications for philosophy, the humanities and the social sciences. In his book *Freud*, Anthony Storr writes: "Freud claimed to be a scientist, and was certainly not a philosopher in the technical sense, nor particularly interested in the subject, although, as a young man, he had translated a book by John Stuart Mill. Nevertheless, he resembled some philosophers in being a system-builder. Very early in its history, psychoanalysis left the narrow confines of the consulting room and made incursions into anthropology, sociology, religion, literature, art and the occult."

For Freud, scientific pursuits were to be strictly separated from therapy. He divided his work into two activities with distinct objectives: firstly, working with patients using free association, i. e. "analyzing"; secondly, scientifically evaluating the observations made during analysis sessions in a "synthetic process of thought". Freud considered psychoanalysis to be a science undergoing continual expansion, and thus it should come as no surprise that he often made multiple revisions of his theories and reworked key texts. In addition to pursuing his theoretical interests in dialog with other physicians and thinkers, Freud made it his goal to institutionalize and anchor the psychoanalytic movement worldwide. He sought out sponsors and at times put his own modest financial resources at stake in getting his works published. First and foremost, he cultivated the International Psychoanalytic Association, recruiting new members and, if necessary, expelling others.

Among Freud's most important scientific influences was Jean-Martin Charcot, under whom he studied on a Paris scholarship in 1885–86. The French neurologist, who was well-known for his hypnosis research at the Salpêtrière, recognized in Freud an extraordinarily gifted student. The encounter with Charcot provided the decisive impulse for Freud's turn away from his area of speciality to date, neurology, and toward psychiatry, even though he continued to practice as a neuropathologist. In 1895 he published, together with Josef Breuer, *Studies on Hysteria*, which marked the beginning of his work on psychoanalysis. In the book, the authors formulated their view, first expressed in 1893, that so-called "hysteria" derived from mental causes and was not a result of physical illness. Until this point in time, patients with pains, breathing difficulties, dizzy spells and other unexplained symptoms were treated for their supposed bodily origins. The ideas of these two Viennese physicians revolutionized the concept of hysteria, which to date had served as a sort of catch-all for a host of disorders.

Shortly after the book's publication, Freud gradually began to withdraw from contact with Breuer, concentrating fully on developing his own theories. Completing and publishing *The Interpretation of Dreams* soon became his primary objective. In this book, he provided for the first time a comprehensive account of the psychoanalytic approach, and it is considered to be the first systematic introduction to the techniques of psychoanalysis. Years later, in 1910 at the psychoanalytic congress in Nuremberg, Freud announced his plans for a complete handbook of the psychoanalytic method. He never realized this plan, however, and thus the basic principles of psychoanalysis were developed in various individually published essays. These works do not provide a thoroughly formulated set of rules on how a psychoanalysis should be conducted; they are conceived as recommendations for the therapeutic treatment of patients.

The only work that could be compared with a textbook in the classic sense is the *Introductory Lectures On Psycho-Analysis*, which Freud held between 1915 and 1917 before students of various faculties at the University of Vienna. These lectures outlining the fundamental theorems of psychoanalysis were published in three editions in 1916 and 1917.

Although it is not a scientific text, the essay "On the History of the Psycho-Analytic Movement" is of central importance in the development of psychoanalysis in a historical sense. Written in 1914, it presents Freud's perspective on the resignation of C. G. Jung as president of the International Psychoanalytic Association and the ensuing schism of the psychoanalytic movement. Freud defends his action toward "dissidents" like Jung, who had once been his introduction into international psychiatric circles, and Alfred Adler, who had been forced to leave the psychoanalytic movement years before. In this polemic writing, Freud claims his exclusive right to define what psychoanalysis is. Jung and Adler continued to see themselves as psychoanalysts, who had simply modified Freud's ideas. In "The History of the Psycho-Analytic Movement" Freud states his position regarding why he refuses them this right, demonstrating the differences between his own theories and those of Adler and Jung – and in his view the weaknesses of the latter.

In 1938 Freud set out to compose a final overview of his theories: the *Outline of Psycho-Analysis*, which remained unfinished, was intended to provide a cogent summary of the work – begun with the 1895 *Studies on Hysteria* – upon which he had spent most of his life. This final writing was published posthumously. Together with *Moses and Monotheism*, a venture into the theory of religion, it can be seen as the legacy that Freud, exhausted after a long battle with cancer and near death, wanted to leave to posterity.

=

"It is not easy to treat feelings scientifically." 1

"Words are malleable material, allowing all kinds of things to be done to them." 2

"The chief patient I am preoccupied with is myself." 3

"We shall never wholly control nature; our constitution, itself part of this nature, will always remain a transient structure, with a limited capacity for adaptation and achievement." 4

5   "Philosophers and students of human nature taught us long ago that we are mistaken in considering our intelligence as an autonomous power, ignoring its dependence upon our emotional lives."

6   "In reality the ego is like the clown in the circus, who is always putting in his oar to make the audience think that whatever happens is his doing."

7   "The theory that there are drives directed at self-preservation, drives that we ascribe to all living beings, stands in striking opposition to the hypothesis that the entire life of the drives serves to procure death."

8   "The goal of all life is death, or to express it retrospectively: the inanimate existed before the animate."

9   "The tension between the stern super-ego and the ego that is subject to it is what we call a 'sense of guilt'; this manifests itself as a need for punishment."

10   "The super-ego is an authority that we postulate, and conscience a function that we ascribe to it – this function being to supervise and assess the actions and intentions of the ego, to exercise a kind of censorship."

11   "The governing rules of logic carry no weight in the unconscious; it might be called the Realm of the Illogical."

"To the oldest of these psychical provinces or agencies we give the name of id. It contains everything that is inherited, that is present at birth, that is laid down in the constitution – above all therefore, the instincts, which originate from the somatic organization and which find a first psychical expression here (in the id) in forms unknown to us." ₁₂

"An action by the ego is as it should be if it satisfies simultaneously the demands of the id, of the super-ego and of reality – that is to say, if it is able to reconcile their demands with one another." ₁₃

"The forces which we assume to exist behind the tensions caused by the needs of the id are called instincts. They represent the somatic demands upon the mind. Though they are the ultimate cause of all activity, they are of a conservative nature; the state, whatever it may be, which an organism has reached gives rise to a tendency to re-establish that state as soon as it has been abandoned." ₁₄

"The death drive becomes the drive to destruction, when it is applied externally, against objects, with the help of certain organs. The organism preserves its own life, so to speak, by destroying that which is strange to it." ₁₅

"Psychoanalysis need not be ashamed if it speaks of love here, because religion says the same thing: love your neighbour as yourself. That is easier said than done. The other kind of emotional bond is the one that comes through identification. Everything that produces significant affinities between hu- ₁₆

man beings produces such shared emotions, such identifica-
tions. A significant part of the structure of human society is
based on them."

17   "It was discovered that people became neurotic because they
could not endure the degree of privation that society imposed on them in the service of its cultural ideals, and it was
inferred that a suspension or a substantial reduction of its demands would mean a return to possibilities of happiness."

18   "Hysterics suffer mainly from reminiscences."

19   "The 'involuntary thoughts' are liable to release a most violent resistance, which seeks to prevent their emergence."

20   "Reality – wish fulfilment: it is from these opposites that our
mental life springs."

21   "It is readily apparent that children repeat everything in their
play that has made a powerful impression on them, and that
in so doing they abreact the intensity of the experience and
make themselves so to speak master of the situation. On the
other hand, however, it is equally clear that all their play is
influenced by the one wish that is dominant at that particular
age: the wish to be grown up, and to be able to do the things
that grown-ups do."

22   "Child psychology, in my opinion, is destined to perform the
same useful services for adult psychology that the investigation of the structure or development of the lower animals

has performed for research into the structure of the higher classes of animals."

"As you know, an explorer's temperament requires two basic qualities: optimism in attempt, criticism in work." 23

"A man who has begun to have an inkling of the grandeur of the universe with all its complexities and its laws readily forgets his own insignificant self." 24

"For I am actually not at all a man of science, not an observer, not an experimenter, not a thinker. I am by temperament nothing but a conquistador – an adventurer, if you will – with all the curiosity, daring, and tenacity characteristic of a man of this sort." 25

"I have not learned enough to be a medical practitioner, and in my medical development there is a flaw which later on was laboriously mended." 26

"I realize that for a doctor work and income are two very different things. Sometimes one makes money without lifting a finger, at other times one slaves away without reward." 27

"As a young man I knew no longing other than for philosophical knowledge, and now I am about to fulfil it as I move from medicine to psychology. I became a therapist against my will; I am convinced that, given certain conditions in regard to the person and the case, I can definitely cure hysteria and obsessional neurosis." 28

29 "Not that I doubt the content of truth in my doctrines, but I find it difficult to believe that they could exert a demonstrable influence on the development of the immediate future."

30 "The teachings of psychoanalysis are based on an incalculable number of observations and experiences, and only someone who has repeated those observations on himself and on others is in a position to arrive at a judgement of his own upon it."

31 "Psychoanalysis was above all an art of interpretation."

32 "Psychoanalysis is like a woman who wants to be seduced but knows she will be underrated unless she offers resistance."

33 "We seek the sober results of research or of reflections founded on research, and we seek to impart to these results no other quality but that of reliability."

34 "It is difficult to practice psychoanalysis in isolation; it is an exquisitely sociable enterprise. It would be so much nicer if we all roared or howled in chorus and in the same rhythm, instead of each one growling to himself in his corner."

35 "Psychoanalysis is justly suspicious. One of its rules is that whatever interrupts the progress of analytic work is a resistance."

"With the neurotics, then, we make our pact: complete cand-   36
our on one side and strict discretion on the other."

"Real sexual relations between patients and analysts are out   37
of the question, and even the subtler methods of satisfaction,
such as the giving of preference, intimacy and so on, are only
sparingly granted by the analyst."

"Psychoanalysis is an instrument to enable the ego to achieve   38
a progressive conquest of the id."

"Although it has been a long time now since I was the only   39
psychoanalyst, I consider myself justified in maintaining that
even today no one can know better than I do what psycho-
analysis is, how it differs from other ways of investigating
the life of the mind, and precisely what should be called psychoanalysis and what should better be described by some
other name."

"During the summer, I should like to go back to anatomy for   40
a while; that is, after all, the only gratifying thing."

"I must confess that I am not at all partial to the fabrication of   41
Weltanschauungen (worldviews). Such activities may be left to
philosophers, who avowedly find it impossible to make their
journey through life without a Baedeker of that kind to give
them information on every subject ... We know well enough
how little light science has so far been able to throw on the
problems that surround us. But however much ado the philosophers may make, they cannot alter the situation. Only pa-

tient, persevering research, in which everything is subordinated to the one requirement of certainty, can gradually bring about a change. The benighted traveller may sing aloud in the dark to deny his own fears; but, for all that, he will not see an inch further beyond his nose."

42 "For the time being psychoanalysis is compatible with various *Weltanschauungen*. But has it yet spoken its last word?"

43 "In view of the kind of matter we work with, it will never be possible to avoid little laboratory explosions."

44 "A proper analysis is a slow process. In some cases I myself have only been able to uncover the core of the problem after many years, not, it is true, of continuous analysis, and I was not able to say where I had gone wrong in my technique."

45 "It is of course of great importance for the progress of the analysis that one should always turn out to be in the right vis-à-vis the patient, otherwise one would always be dependent on what he chose to tell one."

46 "Psychoanalytic activity is arduous and exacting; it cannot well be handled like a pair of glasses that one puts on for reading and takes off when one goes for a walk."

47 "The uninstructed relatives of our patients, who are only impressed by visible and tangible things – preferably by actions of the sort that are to be witnessed at the cinema – never fail to express their doubts whether 'anything can be done about

the illness by mere talking.' That, of course, is both a short-sighted and an inconsistent line of thought. These are the same people who are so certain that patients are 'simply imagining' their symptoms."

"Of all the erroneous and superstitious beliefs of mankind that have supposedly been surmounted, there is not one whose residues do not live on among us today in the lower strata of civilized peoples or even in the highest strata of cultural society. What has once come to life clings tenaciously to its existence. One feels inclined to doubt sometimes whether the dragons of primeval days are really extinct." 48

"My lectures are attended by eleven students who sit there with pencil and paper and hear damnably little that is positive." 49

"A lecture on the etiology of hysteria at the psychiatric society was given an icy reception by the asses and a strange evaluation by Krafft-Ebing: 'It sounds like a scientific fairy tale.' And this, after one has demonstrated to them the solution of a millennia-old problem ...! They can go to hell, euphemistically expressed." 50

"Psychology is really a cross to bear. Bowling or hunting for mushrooms is, in any event, a much healthier pastime." 51

52 "I hope to be well supplied with scientific interests until the end of my life. Apart from that, however, I am scarcely human any longer. By 10:30 in the evening after my practice I am dead tired."

53 "Just as the archaeologist builds up the walls of the building from the foundations that have remained standing, determines the number and position of the columns from depressions, and reconstructs paintings from the remains found in the debris, so does the analyst proceed when he draws inferences from the fragments of memories, from the associations and from the behaviour of the subject of the analysis."

54 "... Do not let us despise the word. After all it is a powerful instrument; it is the means by which we convey our feelings to one another, our method of influencing other people. Words can do unspeakable good and cause terrible wounds. No doubt 'in the beginning was the deed' and the word came later; in some circumstances it meant an advance in civilization when deeds were softened into words. But originally the word was magic, a magical act; and it has retained much of its ancient power."

=

Sources

1 *Civilization*, 2004, p. 2
2 *The Joke*, 2002, p. 27
3 *Freud/Fliess*, 1985, p. 261, 14 Aug. 1897
4 *The Joke*, 2002, p. 29
5 *War and Death*, 2005, p. 181
6 *Freud/Jung*, 1991, p. 219, 1 March 1911
7 *Pleasure Principle*, 2003, p. 79
8 *Pleasure Principle*, 2003, p. 78
9 *Civilization*, 2004, p. 77
10 *Civilization*, 2004, p. 94
11 *An Outline of Psycho-Analysis*, 1961, p. 168 f.
12 *An Outline of Psycho-Analysis*, 1961, p. 145
13 *An Outline of Psycho-Analysis*, 1961, p. 146
14 *An Outline of Psycho-Analysis*, 1961, p. 148
15 *Why War?*, 2005, p. 228
16 *Why War?*, 2005, p. 230
17 *Civilization*, 2004, p. 2
18 *Pleasure Principle*, 2003, p. 51
19 *Dreams*, 1961, p. 102
20 *Freud/Fliess*, 1985, p. 345, 19 Feb. 1899
21 *Pleasure Principle*, 2003, p. 55
22 *Dreams*, 1961, p. 127
23 *Letters*, 1961, p. 108, 21 April 1884, to Martha Bernays
24 *Leonardo Da Vinci*, 1961, p. 77 f.
25 *Freud/Fliess*, 1985, p. 398, 1 Feb. 1900
26 *Freud/Fliess*, 1985, p. 23, 29 Aug. 1888
27 *Letters*, 1961, p. 217, 13 May 1886, to Martha Bernays
28 *Freud/Fliess*, 1985, p. 180, 2 April 1896
29 *Letters*, 1961, p. 429, 18 May 1936, to Stefan Zweig
30 *An Outline of Psycho-Analysis*, 1961, p. 144
31 *Pleasure Principle*, 2003, p. 56
32 *Pleasure Principle*, 2003, p. 77
33 *Letters*, 1961, p. 449, 20 July 1938, to Stefan Zweig
34 *Letters*, 1961, p. 355, 21 Dec. 1924, to Georg Groddeck

35   *Dreams*, 1961, p. 517

36   *An Outline of Psycho-Analysis*, 1961, p. 174

37   *An Outline of Psycho-Analysis*, 1961, p. 176

38   *The Ego and the Id*, 1961, p. 56

39   *History of the Movement*, 1961, p. 7

40   *Freud/Fliess*, 1985, p. 70, 6 May 1894

41   *Inhibitions, Symptoms and Anxiety*, 1961, p. 96

42   *Letters*, 1961, p. 309, 8 July 1915, to James J. Putnam

43   *Freud/Jung*, 1991, p. 154, 18 June 1909

44   *Freud/Zweig*, 1970, p. 107, 13 June 1935

45   *Studies on Hysteria*, 1961, p. 281

46   *New Introductory Lectures*, 1961, p. 152 f.

47   *Introductory Lectures*, 1961, p. 17

48   *Analysis Terminable and Interminable*, 1961, p. 229

49   *Freud/Fliess*, 1985, p. 277, 5 Nov. 1897

50   *Freud/Fliess*, 1985, p. 184, 26 April 1896

51   *Freud/Fliess*, 1985, p. 136, 16 Aug. 1895

52   *Freud/Fliess*, 1985, p. 172, 2 Feb. 1896

53   *Constructions in Analysis*, 1961, p. 259

54   *Lay Analysis*, 1961, p. 187 f.

VIII

WIT AND HUMOUR

"When we are laughing really heartily at a joke, we are not exactly in the most suitable state of mind to inquire into its technique."

J okes are generally told by adults. Sigmund Freud, whose works bear witness to his verbal elan, liked to liven up his writings with jokes, quotes and sarcastic comments. Even in such dry material as his revolutionary theoretical treatise on *The Ego and the Id* (1923), Freud was able to use humour as vehicle for making pure psychoanalytic theory understandable to a wider readership. When Freud sent *The Interpretation of Dreams* to his close friend Wilhelm Fliess and asked his opinion, Fliess remarked that the dreams Freud had used as examples were too humorous. Freud responded in a letter dated 11 September 1899: "All dreamers are equally insufferably witty, and they need to be because they are under pressure, and the direct route is barred to them." Although this statement underlines Freud's pessimistic outlook, one must note that Freud never completely lost his sense of humour – even though at times he only seemed receptive to gallows humour or other darkly cynical quips.

In his cynical remarks he enjoyed invoking the name of his favourite author, Heinrich Heine, who he often found occasion to quote in discussions. More than Heine, however, it was Jewish humour that stocked Freud's extensive collection of jokes. The basic tenor of many of these Jewish jokes is highly self-critical, and a number of them even give rise to feelings of unease today in a post-Holocaust world. Correspondingly, the discourse surrounding Freud's view of the Eastern European Jews is filled with disparate perspectives: Was Freud attempting to distance himself from an oft-derided "immigrant" group to which he himself belonged, or was he paying tribute to the joke tradition of the *fin de siècle*, in which jokes made at the expense of Jews – or Prussians or Bavarians, for instance – were the stock-in-trade of Jewish writers and comedians? In more serious matters, however, Freud showed great solidarity with his Jewish contemporaries, considering his Jewish identity to be something that would always endure the vicissitudes of time.

As a psychoanalyst, Freud saw his repertoire of jokes as more than a private matter and a question of taste: it also provided him with important material for elucidating psychical processes. He was fascinated not only by the mechanisms of jokes and wordplay, but also by what humour hides and disguises, which he attempted to unveil in both the teller and the listener. Even as a young physician, Sigmund Freud had recognized that not only the dream and the *parapraxis* (Freudian slip) must be addressed in research involving human psychopathology, but also the joke. And yet, while *The Interpretation of Dreams* and *The Psychopathology of Everyday Life* are well known to Freud readers worldwide, his 1905 book *Jokes and Their Relation to the Unconscious* has remained in the shadows of the aforementioned works. This comes as a bit of a surprise, inasmuch as the wealth of jokes and humour contained in the work make it attractive to a wider audience. Nevertheless, the book has remained more or less of an "insider tip", in which the father of psychoanalysis reveals his humorous side.

Jokes and humour relate to pleasure. According to Freud, the essence of pleasure is the avoidance of negative feelings.

In no way does the humorist deny the existence of suffering: he merely affects superiority. In his treatise on jokes, Freud evaluates joking as a very "serious" activity of the psyche, which facilitates the satisfaction of an aggressive drive, because it suspends the usual mechanisms of repression and suppression. Pleasure and laughter arise through the sudden negation of psychical agencies of inhibition. In the context of his analysis of jokes, Freud also reaches the conclusion that jokes are to a certain degree a gauge of that which a specific culture suppresses. This is because the joke frees us for a moment from the demands of repression made by civilization. Sexual and aggressive drives are unbridled and for an instant allowed to reach their aim, since jokes make it possible to mercilessly attack the enemy, the underdog, the outsider, to ridicule authority, to break sexual taboos. Freud also focuses on related phenomena of the comic, such as caricature, parody and travesty.

At the same time, Freud recognizes the tenuous nature of jokes: even a minor change in wording or slightly awkward delivery can ruin their effect. A good joke must be brief and succinct, but nonetheless able to capture the hearer's attention through its ambiguity. Freud identifies the coupling of dissimilars, the contrast of ideas and the existence of "sense in nonsense" as decisive techniques of the joke. Although Freud did not make many references to the subject of humour after the publication of his book on jokes in 1905, he continued to collect jokes. Much later, in 1927, he published the paper "Humour", in which he returned his attention to jokes, discussing how they articulate both unbroken rebellion and resignation.

=

"When we are laughing really heartily at a joke, we are not
exactly in the most suitable state of mind to inquire into its
technique." 1

"Money is laughing gas for me." 2

"A physician, leaving a woman's sickbed, shakes his head and
says to her husband accompanying him: 'I don't like the look
of your wife.' – 'I haven't liked the look of her for a long
time,' the husband hastens to agree." 3

"What is a joke to me can be just a comic story to someone
else." 4

"A new joke has almost the same effect as an event of the
widest interest; it is passed from one to another like the news
of the latest victory." 5

"The jokes made about Jews by outsiders are mostly brutal
comic anecdotes, in which (the effort of making) a proper
joke is saved by the fact that to the outsider the Jew counts as
a comical figure." 6

7   "A Galician Jew is travelling on the railway and has made himself very comfortable, unbuttoned his coat, put his feet up on the bench. Then a gentleman in modern dress enters the carriage. At once the Jew pulls himself together, taking up an unobtrusive position in his seat. The stranger turns the pages of a notebook, makes some calculations, thinks, and suddenly turns to the Jew with the question: "Excuse me, when is Yom Kippur?" (Day of Atonement). "Ai-ai-ai," says the Jew, and puts his feet up on the bench again before replying."

8   "A horse dealer is recommending a mount to a client: 'If you take this horse and set off at four in the morning, you'll be in Pressburg at half-past six.' – 'And what am I supposed to be doing in Pressburg at half-past six in the morning?'"

9   "So the technique of the nonsense jokes we have dealt with so far in fact consists in the introduction of something foolish, nonsensical, whose underlying meaning is the illustration, the demonstration, of something else foolish and nonsensical."

10   "On one occasion when he was riding out, Duke Karl of Württemberg happened to meet a dyer who was busied with his trade. 'Can you dye my white horse blue?' the Duke calls out to him, and gets this answer in return: 'Certainly, Your Highness, if he can stand boiling.'"

"Once, when Phokion was applauded after making a speech,
turning to his friends he asked: 'Have I said something foolish?'"

"The *Schadchen (Jewish marriage broker)* is defending the
girl he has suggested in the face of the young man's objec-
tions. 'I don't like the mother-in-law,' the young man says.
'She is a malicious, stupid person.' – 'You're not marrying
the mother-in-law, you're marrying the daughter.' – 'Yes,
but she's no longer so young, and she's not exactly pretty
either.' – 'That doesn't matter. If she's not young and pretty,
she'll be all the more faithful to you.' – 'There is not much
money going, either.' – 'Who's talking about money? Are
you marrying the money? It's a wife you want.' – 'But she's
got a hump-back as well.' – 'Now what are you after? So
she's not to have one single fault?'"

"Of a person who was ambitious, but obdurate in pursuit of
his aims, a friend said: 'He has an ideal in front of his head
(i.e. 'He can't see beyond his ideal')."

"Where a joke is not an end in itself, i.e. innocuous, it puts
itself at the service of two tendencies only, which can themselves be merged into a single viewpoint; it is either a *hostile*
joke (used for aggression, satire, defence) or an *obscene* joke
(used to strip someone naked)."

15 "Among country people or in lower-class taverns, one can observe that it is only when the barmaid or the landlady comes on the scene that the bawdry gets going. The opposite occurs only when we reach a higher social level, and the presence of a female person puts an end to the bawdry; the men save this kind of conversation – which originally presupposed the presence of a woman made ashamed – until they are 'among themselves'."

16 "The greater the disproportion between what is given directly in the joke and what it has necessarily aroused in the listener, the subtler the joke, and the higher it may dare enter into good society."

17 "For every joke demands its own audience, and laughing at the same jokes is evidence of far-reaching psychical compatibility."

18 "The joke will allow us to turn to good account those ridiculous features in our enemy that the obstacles of civility would not let us utter aloud or consciously …"

19 "Anyone who lets the truth slip like this in an unguarded moment is actually glad to be free of the pretence."

20 "We do not dare to talk nonsense; but the inclination characteristic of young boys to get up to absurd and pointless activities seems to me to be the direct issue of pleasure in nonsense."

"In a cheerful mood, most people are, I suppose, capable of pleasantries; the aptitude for making jokes independently of mood is present only in a few." 21

"The joke-work is not at everyone's command, and in general there are only a few who have it in great measure, and we mark them out by saying that they are possessed of 'wit'." 22

"What is a cannibal who has eaten his father and mother? – Answer: An orphan. – And when he has eaten all his other relations as well? – Sole heir. – And where will such a monster find sympathy? – In the dictionary under *S*." 23

"The motive behind the production of innocuous jokes is quite often the ambitious urge to show off how clever one is, to display oneself, a drive to be equated with exhibitionism in the field of sexuality." 24

"When something comic confronts me, I am able to laugh heartily at it by myself – though I am also delighted if I can make someone else laugh by telling him about it. But I am unable to laugh by myself at a joke that has occurred to me, despite the unmistakable enjoyment that it gives me." 25

"To my knowledge, the grimace of drawing back the corners of the mouth in a smile makes its first appearance in the satisfied and surfeited infant as he slips from the breast and falls asleep. There it is an authentic expressive movement, for it tallies with the decision to take in no further nourishment, as 26 it were representing an 'enough'. This original meaning of pleasurable repletion may have imparted to the smile – which after all is still the fundamental manifestation of laughter – its later relation to pleasurable processes of discharge."

27 "Laughter belongs to the highly infectious expressions of psychical states."

28 "A gentleman goes into a pastry-cook's and orders a cake; but he soon brings it back and asks for a glass of liqueur instead. He drinks this up and makes to go off without paying. The shopkeeper detains him. 'What do you want of me?' – 'To pay for the liqueur' – 'But I gave you the cake for it.' – 'You didn't pay for that either.' – *'But I didn't eat it.'*"

29 "The devices for making someone comic are: putting them in comical situations, imitation, disguise, unmasking, caricature, parody, travesty, etc."

30 "First of all one can conjure up the comic in oneself to amuse other people – by pretending to be clumsy or stupid, for example."

31 "A gymnastics instructor or a dancing-master will rarely have an eye for the comedy of movement in his pupils, and the comedy of human weaknesses escapes the clergyman entirely, though the writer of comedies is able to detect it to such great effect."

"A well-known university teacher, who was in the habit of 32
spicing up his not very attractive specialism with jokes, is
congratulated on the birth of his youngest child, granted him
when he was of an already advanced age. 'Yes,' he replied to
his well-wishers, 'it is remarkable what human hand can do.'"

"Children strike us as comic only when they behave not like 33
children but like serious grown-ups, and then they do so in
the same way as other figures who dress up in disguise … On
the other hand, children have no feeling for comedy."

"In our case, when a clear judgement of our own superiority 34
develops, we merely smile instead of laughing …"

"Comic is what is not proper for the grown-ups." 35

"The rogue who is being led to execution on a Monday ex- 36
claims: 'Well, that's a good start to the week.'"

"Jokes and the comic, humour has something liberating about 37
it; but it also has something of grandeur and elevation, which
is lacking in the other two ways of obtaining pleasure from
intellectual activity. The grandeur in it clearly lies in the triumph of narcissism, the victorious assertion of the ego's in-
vulnerability."

38	"The little humour that we come up with ourselves in life is something that as a rule we produce at the cost of annoyance, instead of getting annoyed."

39	"Furthermore, not everyone is capable of the humorous attitude. It is a rare and precious gift, and many people are even without the capacity to enjoy humorous pleasure that is presented to them."

40	"The realm of jokes knows no boundaries."

41	"A man much given to drink earns his living in a little town by coaching pupils. But gradually his vice gets to be known and as a result he loses most of his students. A friend is given the task of urging him to improve his ways. 'Look, you could get the best coaching jobs in town if you gave up drinking. So do it.' – 'Who do you think you are?' comes the indignant answer. 'I coach so that I can drink; am I supposed to give up drinking so that I can get coaching.'"

42	"What an amount of good nature and humour it takes to endure the gruesome business of growing old!"

43	"I should add that I stand in no awe whatever of the Almighty. If we were ever to meet, I should have more reproaches to make to Him than He could to me."

＝

SOURCES

1   *The Joke,* 2002, p. 41
2   *Freud/Fliess,* 1985, p. 375, 21 Sept. 1899
3   *The Joke,* 2002, p. 30
4   *The Joke,* 2002, p. 103
5   *The Joke,* 2002, p. 9
6   *The Joke,* 2002, p. 108 f.
7   *The Joke,* 2002, p. 69
8   *The Joke,* 2002, p. 46
9   *The Joke,* 2002, p. 50
10 *The Joke,* 2002, p. 58
11 *The Joke,* 2002, p. 50
12 *The Joke,* 2002, p. 52
13 *The Joke,* 2002, p. 66
14 *The Joke,* 2002, p. 94
15 *The Joke,* 2002, p. 96 f.
16 *The Joke,* 2002, p. 98
17 *The Joke,* 2002, p. 147
18 *The Joke,* 2002, p. 100
19 *The Joke,* 2002, p. 103
20 *The Joke,* 2002, p. 123
21 *The Joke,* 2002, p. 174
22 *The Joke,* 2002, p. 137
23 *The Joke,* 2002, p. 155
24 *The Joke,* 2002, p. 144
25 *The Joke,* 2002, p. 140 f.
26 *The Joke,* 2002, p. 154
27 *The Joke,* 2002, p. 151
28 *The Joke,* 2002, p. 51
29 *The Joke,* 2002, p. 185
30 *The Joke,* 2002, p. 194
31 *The Joke,* 2002, p. 214

32   *The Joke,* 2002, p. 50

33   *The Joke,* 2002, p. 217

34   *The Joke,* 2002, p. 218

35   *The Joke,* 2002, p. 222

36   *The Joke,* 2002, p. 223

37   *Humour,* 1961, p. 162

38   *The Joke,* 2002, p. 225

39   *Humour,* 1961, p. 166

40   *Dreams,* 1961, p. 176

41   *The Joke,* 2002, p. 44

42   *Letters,* 1961, p. 425, 16 May 1935, to Lou Andreas-Salomé

43   *Letters,* 1961, p. 307 f., 8 July 1915, to James J. Putnam

IX

ET CETERA

"Hardly has the wish for a change been granted when one regrets its fulfilment."

Beyond the insights that arose from his observation of the unconscious and of dreams and from his analysis of himself and others, many of Sigmund Freud's most memorable statements and remarks derive from his everyday life. These in particular reflect his stupendous understanding of human nature and his dry wit. A wide range of themes are addressed in these quips and more extensive comments, ranging from the mood-lifting effects alcohol to a pessimistically coloured definition of happiness: "One has to assume happiness when fate does not carry out all its threats simultaneously." While the quotations garnered from his published writings almost always reflect a theoretically oriented mind and a search for universals, his letters are sometimes permeated with coquettish irony, which in Freud's later years can go so far as to put his entire scientific achievement into question. In his mature years, Freud lamented on various occasions that the future must remain impenetrable to his gaze. Did he fear that his work – to twist the defiant scientific program he set out in quoting Virgil's *Aeneid* – would only move the underworld while remaining unable "to bend the higher powers?" Be that as it may, his regret at being unable to gaze into the future was nourished by his desire to see the scientific territory he had pioneered on so many levels confirmed by future research and technological development. The profound social and technological upheavals that Freud witnessed during his lifetime caused him to address the issue of progress and the concurrent acceleration of life, the haste and rest-lessness of modernity: "The immense extension of communications which has been brought about by the network of telegraphs and telephones that encircle the world has completely altered the conditions of trade and commerce. All is hurry and agitation; night is used for travel, day for business, even 'holiday trips' have become a strain on the nervous system." A combination of fascination and irritation resonate through many of Freud's statements to this effect.

Technological progress and the heightened demands made on the human being in all aspects of work and life pose challenges that – as Freud puts it – the individual can only meet "by putting out all of his mental powers." With great interest, he followed the transformation of urban life occurring in Vienna, the former capital of the Austro-Hungarian Empire, which after the fall of the monarchy was in search of a new identity. The historic city was not immune to the hurriedness and superficiality he perceived in modern life, and he began to feeling increasingly alienated. This sentiment was compounded by his disappointment at his contemporary's dogged adherence to seemingly outmoded patterns of thinking and understanding: "Of all the erroneous and superstitious beliefs of mankind that have supposedly been surmounted, there is not one whose residues do not live on among us today in the lower strata of civilized peoples or even in the highest strata of cultural society. What has once come to life clings tenaciously to its existence. One feels inclined to doubt sometimes whether the dragons of primeval days are really extinct."

Today several of the terms that Freud coined within the framework of his psychoanalytic theory have long since become part of everyday language. In elaborating well-known concepts such as ego, super-ego and id, he made reference not only to his psychoanalytic practice, but also, as a trained medical doctor and a neurologist, drew attention to somatic relationships: "The other agency of the mind, which we believe we know best and in which we recognize ourselves most easily – what is known as the ego – has developed out of the id's cortical layer, which, through being adapted to the reception and exclusion of stimuli, is in direct contact with the external world (reality)."

Freud did not attempt to conceal the speculative, and at times fragmentary, nature of some of his theories. Although many of his research findings – for example those relating to his theory of drives – could be confirmed theoretically, they did not always produce successful results in therapeutic application. Toward the end of his life, many of Freud's statements carry an undertone of resignation: "Passions that derive from the drives are stronger than reasonable interests." The darkening political situation clouded the late recognition of his life's work, as is revealed in a letter to Arnold Zweig dated 31 May 1936, in which he comments on the celebration of his eightieth birthday: "Even the Viennese colleagues celebrated me and betrayed by all manner of signs how difficult they found it. The Minister of Education sent a formal message of polite congratulation, whereupon the newspapers were forbidden on pain of confiscation to publish this act of sympathy within the country. Foreign and domestic newspapers printed numerous articles expressing hatred and repudiation."

===

"Hardly has the wish for a change been granted when one regrets its fulfilment." 1

"It still remains surprising to me how little we human beings can foresee the future." 2

"Altering our state of mind is the most valuable thing that alcohol has done for humankind, and that is why this 'poison' is not equally indispensable for everyone." 3

"Under the influence of alcohol the adult becomes a child again, finding pleasure in having the course of his thoughts freely at his disposal without having to keep to the compulsion of logic." 4

"The extraordinary achievements of modern times, the discoveries and inventions in every sphere, the maintenance of progress in the face of increasing competition – these things have only been gained, and can only be held, by great mental effort." 5

6   "The immense extension of communications which has been brought about by the network of telegraphs and telephones that encircle the world has completely altered the conditions of trade and commerce. All is hurry and agitation; night is used for travel, day for business, even 'holiday trips' have become a strain on the nervous system."

7   "City life is constantly becoming more sophisticated and more restless."

8   "The demands made on the efficiency of the individual in the struggle for existence have greatly increased, and it is only by putting out all his mental powers that he can meet them."

9   "The ideal condition ... would be a community of people who have subjected their drives to the dictatorship of reason."

10 "The feeling of happiness resulting from the satisfaction of a wild instinctual impulse that has not been tamed by the ego is incomparably more intense than that occasioned by the sating of one that has been tamed. Here we have an economic explanation for the irresistibility of perverse impulses, perhaps for the attraction of whatever is forbidden."

11 "Nothing protects virtue as securely as an illness."

12 "An image comes disagreeably to mind, of mills that grind so slowly that people might starve before they had their flour."

"Oh, life could be very interesting if we only knew and understood more about it." 13

"If the energy I feel within me remains with me, we may yet leave behind us some traces of our complicated existence." 14

"I am one of Vienna's greatest philanthropists! I pay 1,500 gulden every year to the poor. I am also one of the most pious Jews: it is only at Passover that the pious put out a chair and a cup for Elihanovi, who never comes; and I have fixed up a whole room for him. I wouldn't know who else my waiting room is for." 15

"While I was in the next room, I heard a child who was afraid of the dark call out: 'Do speak to me, Auntie! I'm frightened!' – 'Why, what good would that do? You can't see me.' To this the child replied: 'If someone speaks, it gets lighter.' Thus a longing felt in the dark is transformed into a fear of the dark." 16

"People's phantasies are less easy to observe than the play of children." 17

"Holding back aggression is in general unhealthy and leads to illness (to mortification). A person in a fit of rage will often demonstrate how the transition from hindered aggression to self-destructiveness is brought about by diverting the aggression against himself: he tears his hair or beats his face with his fists, though he would evidently have preferred to apply this treatment to someone else." 18

19 "Against all the evidence of the senses, the person in love asserts that 'I' and 'you' are one and is ready to behave as if this were so."

20 "A joke will fall flat at the second time of hearing; a play will never again make the same impression that it did on first viewing; indeed it would be difficult to get an adult to re-read a much-enjoyed book until considerable time had elapsed. Novelty will always be the precondition of enjoyment. The child, however, will never tire of requiring adults to repeat a game that they showed him or played with him, until they refuse out of sheer exhaustion. And once anyone has told him a nice story, he wants to hear the same story again and again rather than a new one; he implacably insists that every repetition be exactly the same; and he corrects every least change that the story-teller misguidedly incorporates, perhaps fondly imagining it will gain him extra kudos."

21 "Passions that derive from the drives are stronger than reasonable interests."

22 "An etching which Schmutzer *(a Viennese portraitist)* completed for the birthday strikes me as excellent. Others find its expression too severe, almost angry. Inwardly this is probably what I am."

23 "It seems a completely unrealistic notion to send women into the struggle for existence in the same way as men."

"We must link our lives to those of others in such a way, we   24
must be able to identify with others so closely, that we are
able to overcome the curtailment of our own lifetime; and we
may not fulfil the demands of our own needs illegitimately,
but must leave them unfulfilled, because only the continued
existence of so many unfulfilled demands is able to develop
the power to change the social order."

"One has to assume happiness when fate does not carry out   25
all its threats simultaneously."

=

Sources

1   *Letters,* 1961, p. 334 f., 4 Aug. 1921, to Oscar Rie
2   *Letters,* 1961, p. 457, 7 March 1939, to Ernest Jones
3   *The Joke,* 2002, p. 124
4   *The Joke,* 2002, p. 124
5   *Sexual Morality,* 1961, p. 183
6   *Sexual Morality,* 1961, p. 183
7   *Sexual Morality,* 1961, p. 183
8   *Sexual Morality,* 1961, p. 183
9   *Why War?,* 2005, p. 230
10 *Civilization,* 2004, p. 20
11 *Sexual Morality,* 1961, p. 195
12 *Why War?,* 2005, p. 230
13 *Letters,* 1961, p. 40, 8 May 1932, to Arnold Zweig
14 *Letters,* 1961, p. 158, 26 June 1885, to Martha Bernays
15 *Freud/Minna Bernays,* 2005, p. 172, 24 Oct. 1886
16 *Introductory Lectures,* 1961, p. 407

17 *Creative Writers,* 1961, p. 145

18 *An Outline of Psycho-Analysis,* 1961, p. 150

19 *Civilization,* 2004, p. 3.

20 *Pleasure Principle,* 2003, p. 75 f.

21 *Civilization,* 2004, p. 61

22 *Letters,* 1961, p. 369, 10 May 1926, to Marie Bonaparte

23 *Letters,* 1961, p. 76, 15 Nov. 1883, to Martha Bernays

24 *The Joke,* 2002, p. 107

25 *Freud/Fliess,* 1985, p. 440, 24 March 1901

X
Cult and Religion

"Long ago he *(Man)* formed an ideal conception of omnipotence and omniscience, which he embodied in his gods, attributing to them whatever seemed beyond the reach of his desires — or was forbidden him. We may say, then, that these gods were cultural ideals."

Throughout his lifetime, Freud returned repeatedly to the critical investigation of cult and religion. Primarily, he attempted to reduce religion to a system of doctrines and promises. According to Freud, religion's claim to offer a complete explanation of the mysteries of our world corresponds to an infantile helplessness, and a father yearning developed by the religious to compensate for it. Furthermore, Freud recognized collective and individual feelings of guilt as an important component in the genesis of religion. By promising liberation from guilt feelings, religion elevated guilt to a religious-moral category through the concept of sin.

Here Freud is thinking not only of Christian redemption theology, but also of Judaism and the Old Covenant: "The people of Israel had thought of itself as God's favourite child, and when the great Father let one misfortune after another rain down upon His people, it never doubted this relationship with God or questioned His power and justice, but brought forth the prophets, who reproached it for its sinfulness, and created, from its consciousness of guilt, the exceedingly stern precepts of its priestly religion." Freud sees religion primarily as obsessional neurosis and wish fantasy. Consequently, he considers the question of human life's purpose, as instrumentalized by the various religions, to be an undertaking promising little success: "... It seems that one is entitled to dismiss the question," he writes in the 1930 book *Civilization and Its Discontents*. Every human being must find his or her own path, discovering and fulfilling his or her own aims in life. The tenor of Freud's critique of religion is primarily that it forces everyone to follow the same path, and that it cannot deliver on its promises.

Among the latter is the belief in the hereafter, which Freud sees as a product of the enduring memory of the dead, elaborated by religion into an "afterlife more desirable and truly valid" than this one. From the painful experience of a beloved person's death, Freud derives not only "the theory of souls, belief in immortality and a powerful root for the human sense of guilt, but also the first ethical commandments. The first and most significant prohibition of the awakening conscience was: *Thou shalt not kill*."

In this context Freud also criticizes the ideal of Christian altruism as it is pointedly formulated in the New Testament: "Thou shalt love thy neighbour as thyself." Beyond noting that this injunction predates Christianity, Freud draws attention to the fact that human beings, on account of their limited resources, are unable to include all others in their love. Our love of our true friends would be depreciated if it had to be generalized to include every other human being. Thus Freud would like to replace this dictum with the injunction: "Love thy neighbour as thy neighbour loves thee."

Freud's experience of religion came primarily from Judaism, to which he professed an affiliation, although he made no bones about being an atheist. This ambivalence is captured in two Freud quotations presented here. In a letter to Charles Singer from October 1938, Freud noted: "Neither in my private life nor in my writings have I ever made a secret of my being an out-and-out unbeliever." And yet, in a revealing statement made in his 1925 "Autobiographical Study", he confessed: "My deep engrossment in the Bible story (almost as soon as I had learnt the art of reading) had, as I recognized much later, an enduring effect upon the direction of my interest." In his last work, *Moses and Monotheism*, which was published in 1939, Freud put aside his atheism in expressing his approval of Judaism, which through its strict commandments in renunciation of drives and its "dematerialized" God achieved a "triumph of intellectuality over sensuality." Many of his earlier works also deal with biblical themes – for example, when he cites the "Fall" in contrasting drive and intellect, using it to derive his ideas concerning the latent tension between consciousness and animality, or between knowledge and shame.

All in all, Freud's writings display an ambivalent attitude toward religion. Despite his atheist orientation, he admitted that religion played an important role in the renunciation of drives, which was a condition for the development of a higher degree of intellectuality. He views the conscience, for example, as a product of drive renunciation. In many of his statements, Freud shows considerable understanding for the human search for relief and solace from life's inevitable sorrows. Thus his central argument against religion is targeted not at its catalogue of prohibitions against living out the needs imposed by instinct, but at excessive moralizing and at the impediments to free thought posed by religion.

=

"Long ago he *(Man)* formed an ideal conception of omnipo- 1
tence and omniscience, which he embodied in his gods, attributing to them whatever seemed beyond the reach of his
desires – or was forbidden him. We may say, then, that these
gods were cultural ideals."

"To me the derivation of religious needs from the helpless- 2
ness of the child and a longing for its father seems irrefutable,
especially as this feeling is not only prolonged from the days
of childhood, but constantly sustained by a fear of the super-
ior power of fate."

"Everyone must discover for himself how he can achieve sal- 3
vation."

"One is inclined to say that the intention that Man should be 4
'happy' has no part in the plan of 'creation'."

"If the believer is finally obliged to speak of God's 'inscrut- 5
able decrees', he is admitting that all he has left to him, as
the ultimate consolation and source of pleasure in the midst
of suffering, is unconditional submission. And if he is ready
to accept this, he could probably have spared himself the de-
tour."

"The question of the purpose of human life has been posed 6
innumerable times; it has not yet received a satisfactory answer and perhaps does not admit of one. Some of those who
have posed it have added that if life should turn out to have
no purpose, it would lose any value it had for them. Yet this

threat alters nothing. Rather, it seems that one is entitled to dismiss the question."

7 "It can hardly be wrong to conclude that the notion that life has a purpose stands or falls with the religious system."

8 "So long as things go well for a person, his conscience is lenient and indulges the ego in all kinds of ways. When a misfortune has befallen him, he searches his soul, recognizes his sinfulness, pitches the demands of his conscience higher, imposes privations on himself, and punishes himself by acts of penance."

9 "The hermit turns his back on the world and refuses to have anything to do with it. But one can do more than this: one can try to re-create the world, to build another in its place, one in which the most intolerable features are eliminated and replaced by others that accord with one's desires."

10 "The religions, at least, have never ignored the part that a sense of guilt plays in civilization … They claim to redeem humanity from this sense of guilt, which they call sin. From the way in which this redemption is achieved in Christianity – through the sacrificial death of one man, who thereby takes upon himself the guilt shared by all – we drew an inference as to what may have been the original occasion for our acquiring this primordial guilt, which also marked the beginning of civilization."

"Conscience results from the renunciation of the drives, or that this renunciation (imposed on us from without) creates the conscience, which then demands further renunciation." 11

"We cannot get away from the assumption that the sense of guilt stems from the Oedipus complex and was acquired when the brothers banded together and killed the father." 12

"We human beings are rooted in our animal nature and could never become godlike. The earth is a small planet, not suited to be a 'heaven'." 13

"This is where ethics based on religion enters the scene with its promises of a better life hereafter. I am inclined to think, for as long as virtue goes unrewarded here below, ethics will preach in vain." 14

"The self-judgement which declares that the ego falls short of its ideal produces the religious sense of humility to which the believer appeals in his longing." 15

"But even ordinary normal morality has a harshly restraining, cruelly prohibiting quality. It is from this, indeed, that the conception arises of a higher being who deals out punishment inexorably." 16

"... Our conscience is not the inflexible judge that ethicists claim it to be; it is by origin 'social anxiety' and nothing else. Where the community ceases to accuse, the suppression of evil desires is also abolished, and people commit deeds of 17 cruelty, cunning, treachery and barbarism, the possibility of which one would have considered irreconcilable with their level of civilization."

18 "Finally, what good is a long life to us if it is hard, joyless and so full of suffering that we can only welcome death as a deliverer?"

19 "Fundamentally no one believes in his own death or, which comes to the same thing: in the unconscious each of us is convinced of his immortality."

20 "The constant memory of the dead person became the foundation of the hypothesis of other forms of life, and first gave rise to the idea of life continuing after apparent death. At first these later existences were only supplements to the one ended by death, shadowy, lacking in content and held in low esteem ... Only later did the religions come to represent this afterlife as being more desirable and truly valid, and to reduce the life ended by death to a mere preparation."

21 "What came into being by the side of the loved one's corpse was not only the theory of souls, belief in immortality and a powerful root for the human sense of guilt, but also the first ethical commandments. The first and most significant prohibition of the awakening conscience was: *Thou shalt not kill*."

"If God's son had to sacrifice his life to free humanity from   22
original sin, then according to the law of talion – the recom-
pense of like by like – that sin must have been a killing, a
murder. That alone could require as its expiation the sacrifice
of a life. And if original sin was an offence against God the
father, then humanity's oldest crime must have been a patri-
cide, the killing of the primal father of the primitive human
horde, whose memory-image was later transfigured into a
deity."

"After St. Paul had made universal brotherly love the found-   23
ation of his Christian community, the extreme intolerance of
Christianity towards those left outside it was an inevitable
consequence."

"My judgement of human nature, above all the Christian-   24
Aryan variety, has had little reason to change."

"And here I should like to add that I do not think our cures   25
can compete with those of Lourdes. There are so many more
people who believe in the miracles of the Blessed Virgin than
in the existence of the unconscious."

"The Devil would be the best excuse for God; he would take   26
on the same exculpatory role in this context as the Jew in the
world of the Aryan ideal. But even so, one can still demand
that God be held responsible for the existence of the Devil
and the evil he embodies."

27   "The people of Israel had thought of itself as God's favourite
      child, and when the great Father let one misfortune after an-
      other rain down upon His people, it never doubted this rela-
      tionship with God or questioned His power and justice, but
      brought forth the prophets, who reproached it for its sinful-
      ness, and created, from its consciousness of guilt, the exceed-
      ingly stern precepts of its priestly religion."

28   "I was born on May 6th, 1856, at Freiberg in Moravia, a small
      town in what is now Czechoslovakia. My parents were Jews,
      and I have remained a Jew myself."

29   "I may have been ten or twelve years old, when my father
      began to take me with him on his walks and reveal to me in
      his talk his views upon things in the world we live in. Thus
      it was, on one such occasion, that he told me a story to show
      me how much better things were now than they had been
      in his days. 'When I was a young man,' he said, 'I went for
      a walk one Saturday in the streets of your birthplace; I was
      well dressed, and had a new fur cap on my head. A Chris-
      tian came up to me and with a single blow knocked off my
      cap into the mud, shouting: 'Jew! Get off the pavement!' –
      'And what did you do?' I asked. 'I went into the roadway and
      picked up my cap,' was his quiet reply. This struck me as un-
      heroic conduct on the part of the big, strong man who was
      holding the little boy by the hand."

30   "What tied me to Jewry was – I have to admit it – not the
      faith, not even the national pride, for I was always an un-
      believer, having been brought up without religion, but not

without respect for the so-called 'ethical' demands of human civilization."

"Faced with the renewed persecutions, one asks oneself again how the Jew came to be what he is and why he has drawn upon himself this undying hatred." 31

"Nor is it perhaps entirely a matter of chance that the first advocate of psychoanalysis was a Jew. To profess belief in this new theory called for a certain degree of readiness to accept a situation of solitary opposition – a situation with which no one is more familiar than a Jew." 32

"If it is the prerogative of the Lord that the millennia pass for Him like the blink of an eye, we humans wallow in the opposite: days seem to us like millennia. It is a devilish situation: torment makes the time long, joy makes it short." 33

"The prohibition against thought issued by religion to assist in its self-preservation is also far from being free of danger, either for the individual or for human society." 34

(on the death of daughter Sophie) 35
"For years I have been bracing myself for the death of a son, and now it has struck my daughter. Since I am at my deepest an unbeliever, I have no one to blame, and I know that there is no place I could assail with my grief."

"Neither in my private life nor in my writings have I ever made a secret of my being an out-and-out unbeliever." 36

37   "It is certainly foolish to want to banish suffering and dying from the world ... and this is not why we did away with our dear Lord God, only to lift them both from us and from our dear ones and dump them on strangers."

=

SOURCES

1   *Civilization*, 2004, p. 36
2   *Civilization*, 2004, p. 11
3   *Civilization*, 2004, p. 26
4   *Civilization*, 2004, p. 16
5   *Civilization*, 2004, p. 28
6   *Civilization*, 2004, p. 15
7   *Civilization*, 2004, p. 16
8   *Civilization*, 2004, p. 80
9   *Civilization*, 2004, p. 28
10   *Civilization*, 2004, p. 93
11   *Civilization*, 2004, p. 83
12   *Civilization*, 2004, p. 86
13   *Letters*, 1961, p. 384, 9 Dec. 1928, to Richard Dyer-Bennett
14   *Civilization*, 2004, p. 103 f.
15   *The Ego and the Id*, 1961, p. 37
16   *The Ego and the Id*, 1961, p. 54
17   *War and Death*, 2005, p. 174
18   *Civilization*, 2004, p. 32
19   *War and Death*, 2005, p. 183
20   *War and Death*, 2005, p. 188 f.
21   *War and Death*, 2005, p. 189
22   *War and Death*, 2005, p. 187
23   *Civilization*, 2004, p. 65
24   *Letters*, 1961, p. 418, 28 May 1933, to Oscar Pfister
25   *New Introductory Lectures*, 1961, p. 152

26 *Civilization*, 2004, p. 72

27 *Civilization*, 2004, p. 81

28 *An Autobiographical Study*, 1961, p. 7

29 *Dreams*, 1961, p. 197

30 *Letters*, 1961, p. 366, 6 May 1926, to the members of the B'nai B'rith Lodge

31 *Letters*, 1961, p. 421, 30 Sept. 1934, to Arnold Zweig

32 *Resistances*, 1961, p. 222

33 *Freud/Minna Bernays*, 2005, p. 85, 23 Aug. 1883

34 *New Introductory Lectures*, 1961, p. 171

35 *Briefe*, 1968, p. 346, 19 April 1920, to Sandor Ferenczi

36 *Letters*, 1961, p. 453, 31 Oct. 1938, to Charles Singer

37 *Freud/Fliess*, 1985, p. 442 f., 9 June 1901

Appendix

1856 Sigismund Schlomo Freud is born on 6 May in Freiberg, Moravia (now Příbor in the Czech Republic).

1860 The Freuds move to Vienna.

1873 Sigmund Freud finishes his schooling at the *Gymnasium* and enters Vienna University.

1881 Sigmund Freud qualifies as doctor of medicine.

1882–1883 Freud is employed as a doctor in Theodor
Meynert's psychiatric clinic.

1884–1885 Studies of the medicinal effects of coca.

1885–1886 Five-month study grant at the Paris Salpêtrière
Hospital under Jean-Martin Charcot, who awakens
Freud's interest in the therapeutic use of hypnosis.

1886 Marriage to Martha Bernays. Between 1887 and 1895
the family's six children are born (Mathilde, Martin,
Oliver, Ernst, Sophie and Anna). Freud goes into
private medical practice.

1891 Move to Berggasse 19.

1895 Together with Joseph Breuer, Freud publishes the
Studies on Hysteria. During the same year he also
succeeds for the first time in interpreting one of his
own dreams.

1896 Freud's first use of the term "psychoanalysis".

1897 Freud begins his self-analysis.

1899 The first copies of *The Interpretation of Dreams* are
delivered, post-dated 1900.

1901 Freud begins the analysis of the eighteen-year-old
"Dora".

1902 Sigmund Freud is appointed Professor at the University of Vienna. Founding of the Wednesday Psychological Society.

1905 *Three Essays on the Theory of Sexuality, Jokes and Their Relation to the Unconscious* and "Fragment of an Analysis of a Case of Hysteria" ("Dora") are published.

1906 C. G. Jung begins his correspondence with Freud.

1907 Publication of "Delusion and Dreams in W. Jensen's Gradiva" and "Creative Writers and Day-Dreaming".

1908 The First Congress of "Freudian Psychology" takes place in Salzburg. Publication of "'Civilized' Sexual Morality and Modern Nervous Illness".

1910 Founding of the International Psychoanalytic Association.

1911 Alfred Adler resigns from the Vienna Psychoanalytic Society.

1912 Founding of the psychoanalytic journal *Imago*.

1913 Break with C. G. Jung. Publication of *Totem and Taboo*.

1914 Publication of the polemical "History of the Psycho-Analytic Movement" and of "The Moses of Michelangelo".

1915 Freud writes "Timely Reflections on War and Death" around six months after the outbreak of the First World War.

1916 The first part of the *Introductory Lectures on Psycho-Analysis* is published.

1918 Freud begins the analysis of his daughter Anna.

1919 Founding of the International Psychoanalytic Press in Vienna.

1920 Freud's daughter Sophie dies in the Hamburg influenza epidemic. Founding of the English language *International Journal of Psycho-Analysis*. Publication of *Beyond the Pleasure Principle*.

1921 Publication of *Group Psychology and the Analysis of the Ego*.

1923 The first signs of Freud's oral cancer are detected. Publication of *The Ego and the Id*.

1925 Publication of "An Autobiographical Study".

1926 Quackery charges levelled at a young analyst inspire Freud to write *The Question of Lay Analysis*.

1927 Freud publishes *The Future of an Illusion*, a psychoanalytic assault on religion.

1930 Publication of *Civilization and Its Discontents*.

1933 Freud corresponds with Einstein on the question "Why War?". Publication of the *New Introductory Lectures on Psycho-Analysis*.

1935 Freud is elected Honorary Member of the British Royal Society of Medicine.

1938 The Freud apartment is searched by the Gestapo; Anna Freud is detained for a day and interrogated. All psychoanalytic institutions are forced to close. Sigmund Freud emigrates with his family to London.

1939 Sigmund Freud dies on 23 September in London. Publication of *Moses and Monotheism*.

Works

SIGMUND FREUD, *The Standard Edition of the Complete Psychological Works of Sigmund Freud*, ed. and trans. by James Strachey, Hogarth Press, London, 1961. Reprinted by permission of The Random House Group Ltd.

Studies on Hysteria, with Josef Breuer (1895), vol. II

The Interpretation of Dreams (1900), vols. IV/V

Jokes and Their Relation to the Unconscious (1905), vol. VIII

"'Civilized' Sexual Morality and Modern Nervous Illness" (1908), vol. IX

"Creative Writers and Day-Dreaming" (1908), vol. IX

"Leonardo da Vinci and a Memory of his Childhood" (1910), vol. XI

"On the History of the Psycho-Analytic Movement" (1914), vol. XIV

Introductory Lectures on Psycho-Analysis (1915–17), vols. XV/XVI

The Ego and the Id (1923), vol. XIX

"An Autobiographical Study" (1925), vol. XX

"The Resistances to Psycho-Analysis" (1925), vol. XIX

Inhibitions, Symptoms and Anxiety (1926), vol. XX

The Question of Lay Analysis (1926), vol. XX

"Humour" (1927), vol. XXI

Civilization and Its Discontents (1930), vol. XXI

New Introductory Lectures on Psycho-Analysis (1933–36), vol. XXII

"Analysis Terminable and Interminable" (1937), vol. XXIII

"Constructions in Analysis" (1937), vol. XXIII

An Outline of Psycho-Analysis (1940), vol. XXIII

—, *The Joke and Its Relation to the Unconscious* (1905), trans. Joyce Crick, Penguin Books, London, 2002.

—, *Beyond the Pleasure Principle* (1920), in Sigmund Freud, *Beyond the Pleasure Principle and Other Writings*, trans. John Reddick, Penguin Books, London, 2003.

—, *Civilization and Its Discontents* (1930), trans. David McLintock, Penguin Books, London, 2004.

—, "Timely Reflections on War and Death" (1915), in Sigmund Freud, *On Murder, Mourning and Melancholia*, trans. Shaun Whiteside, Penguin Books, London, 2005.

—, "Why War?" (1933), in Sigmund Freud, *On Murder, Mourning and Melancholia*, trans. Shaun Whiteside, Penguin Books, London, 2005.

Letters

ERNST L. FREUD (ed.), *The Letters of Sigmund Freud*, trans. Tania and James Stern, Basic Books, New York, 1961.

ERNST AND LUCIE FREUD (eds.), *Sigmund Freud, Briefe 1873–1939*, second expanded edition, Fischer Verlag, Frankfurt, 1968.

ERNST L. FREUD (ed.), *The Letters of Sigmund Freud and Arnold Zweig*, trans. Prof. and Mrs. W. D. Robson-Scott, Hogarth Press, London, 1970.

JEFFREY MOUSSAIEFF MASSON (ed. and trans.), *The Complete Letters of Sigmund Freud to Wilhelm Fliess*, Harvard University Press, Cambridge, Mass., 1985.

WALTER BOEHLICH (ed.), *The Letters of Sigmund Freud to Eduard Siberstein*, trans. Arnold J. Pemerans, Belknap Press, Cambridge, Mass., 1990.

WILLIAM MCGUIRE (ed.), *The Freud/Jung Letters*, trans. Ralph Manheim and R. C. F. Hull, Penguin Books, London, 1991.

EVA BRABANT, ERNST FALZEDER, PARTRIZIA GIAMPIERI-DEUTSCH (eds.), *The Correspondence of Sigmund Freud and Sandor Ferenczi*, trans. Peter T. Hoffer, Belknap Press, Cambridge, Mass., 1993.

ALBRECHT HIRSCHMÜLLER (ed.), *Sigmund Freud/Minna Bernays: Briefwechsel 1882–1938*, Edition Diskord, Tübingen, 2005.

MICHAEL SCHRÖTER (ed.), *Sigmund Freud – Unterdess halten wir zusammen: Briefe an die Kinder*, Aufbau Verlag, Berlin, 2010.

Translator's note: Occasionally the wording of an existing translation has been modified slightly to improve readability or to conform with modern usage.

page 17: Sigmund Freud, photographed by Max Halberstadt, 1921. © IMAGNO/Sigmund Freud Copyrights London.

page 33: Sigmund Freud at the Sixth International Psychoanalytic Congress in The Hague, 1920. © IMAGNO/Sigmund Freud Foundation.

page 45: Sigmund Freud, reading a newspaper, Hochrotherd in the Vienna Woods, 1932. © IMAGNO/Sigmund Freud Foundation.

page 59: Sigmund Freud with his son Martin home from the Front, 1916. © IMAGNO/Sigmund Freud Foundation.

page 75: Liège, object by Franz West, 1989. © Gerald Zugmann.

page 91: Martha Bernays, ca. 1885. © IMAGNO/Sigmund Freud Foundation.

page 107: Sigmund Freud in London working on the manuscript of *Moses and Monotheism*, 1938. © IMAGNO/Sigmund Freud Foundation.

page 125: Sigmund Freud with his daughter Anna in den Dolomites, 1913. © IMAGNO/Austrian Archives.

page 141: Sigmund Freud, photographed by Max Halberstadt, ca. 1930. © IMAGNO/Sigmund Freud Copyrights London.

page 153: Aphrodite, Late Hellenistic statuette from Sigmund Freud's collection, 1st or 2nd century BC, Asia Minor. © Sigmund Freud Foundation.

page 167: Marie Bonaparte with Sigmund and Martha Freud in Paris, 1938. © IMAGNO/Sigmund Freud Foundation.

The Authors

HANNES ETZLSTORFER, born 1959 in Lasberg (Upper Austria). Studied art history, theatre and theology in Vienna. As an art and cultural historian, exhibition curator and culture journalist, he has participated in more than eighty exhibitions on in Austria and abroad. He has authored and edited numerous books and catalogues on themes related to art, cultural and social history. His work on the subject of Sigmund Freud has intensified in recent years, partly on account of the 2009 exhibition *Eros and Thanatos* at the Sigmund Freud Museum and Liechtenstein Museum in Vienna, for which he served as co-curator.

PETER NÖMAIER, born 1980 in Ried/Innkreis (Upper Austria). Studied journalism and political science in Vienna. After graduation he worked as a public relations consultant for businesses and cultural institutions. Since 2006 he has been the press officer of the Sigmund Freud Museum, and since 2008 he has served there in other administrative capacities as well. He has published several texts on the life and work of Sigmund Freud.

INGE SCHOLZ-STRASSER, Director of the Sigmund Freud Museum in Vienna. Studied history and philosophy in Vienna. She has published numerous works on the theory and history of psychoanalysis. Together with Peter Pakesch and Joseph

Kosuth she initiated the conceptual art collection "Foundation for the Arts, Sigmund Freud Museum Vienna", and she has curated numerous exhibitions on art and psychoanalysis in Austria and abroad. From 1987 to 2005 she served as Secretary General of the Sigmund Freud Society, and since 2003 she has been Chairwoman of the Sigmund Freud Foundation, which administrates the museum as well as its archive and research library.